Haunted Georgia

Ghosts and Strange Phenomena of the Peach State

Alan Brown

Illustrations by Heather Adel Wiggins

STACKPOLE BOOKS

Published in 2008 by
STACKPOLE BOOKS
5067 Ritter Road
Mechanicsburg, PA 17055
www.stackpolebooks.com

FIRST EDITION

Cover design by Caroline Stover
Illustrations by Heather Adel Wiggins

Library of Congress Cataloging-in-Publication Data

Brown, Alan, 1950 Jan. 12-
    Haunted Georgia : ghosts and strange phenomena of the Peach State /
Alan Brown. — 1st ed.

        p.   cm.
    Includes bibliographical references (p.).
    ISBN-13: 978-0-8117-3443-1 (pbk.)
    ISBN-10: 0-8117-3443-9 (pbk.)
    1. Haunted places—Georgia. 2. Ghosts—Georgia. I. Title.
BF1472.U6B7425   2008
133.109758—dc22
                                                        2007025887

Contents

Contents

Introduction

WHEN THE UNIVERSITY PRESS OF MISSISSIPPI ASKED ME TO WRITE *Ghost Hunters of the South,* I had only a very general knowledge of Georgia's haunted past. I had been to Savannah on a ghost story collecting trip in 2002, but I had little knowledge of Georgia's other haunted places. When I began interviewing the directors of ghost-hunting groups throughout the South, however, my opinion of Georgia as a repository of ghost stories changed considerably. More Georgia ghost-hunting groups—eight—agreed to be included in my book than any other southern groups. Before long, names like Anthony's Restaurant and Tunnel Hill were added to my personal list of America's most haunted places. Several of these groups were so knowledgeable of Georgia's haunted history that I asked them to assist me with the writing of *Haunted Georgia.* Naturally, I began wondering why Georgia has so many ghost stories, aside from the fact that it is the largest state east of the Mississippi River. This book was written in an attempt to answer that question.

According to Troy Taylor in *The Ghost Hunter's Guidebook,* the spirits of some deceased individuals linger on in our own world because of murder, a traumatic event, or emotions that tie them to earth. Looking over these stories, I have found three historic events that could have produced the kind of trauma that results in hauntings in Georgia. The first is piracy. Pirates, strictly speaking, were individuals who committed acts of robbery on the high seas. In the eighteenth century, pirates were welcome in coastal towns in North and South Carolina as long as they preyed on Spanish ships. Some found a home in Savannah. Pirates from as far away as the Red Sea and Madagascar swaggered around the docks, looking for rum and women. In fact, Savannah was so associated with piracy in the early days that the city is mentioned several times in Robert Louis Stevenson's novel *Treasure Island.* The best known of Savannah's pirates, Captain Flint, is said to have been the model for Long John Silver. Legend has it that the drunken pirate died in an upstairs room of the Pirate's House.

By the time Georgia had become a colony in 1734, the Golden Age of Piracy was practically over. The invention of the steam engine and the growth of the British and American navies in the late eighteenth and early nineteenth centuries seriously reduced the threat of piracy to people living and working along America's coastline. Conventional pirates were replaced by privateers, who robbed merchant ships for the good of a patron nation. The most famous American privateer, Jean Lafitte, had more than a hundred pirates under his command. He was instrumental in preventing the United States from losing control of the city of New Orleans in the War of 1812. Lafitte too is said to have visited Georgia on occasion. The violence perpetrated by cutthroats like Black Dog and Billy Bones lives on in the ghost tales of Georgia, especially in cities along the coast.

Another historic event that generated countless ghost stories in Georgia is slavery. Ironically, the Georgia Trustees who drew up plans for the Colonial experiment in Georgia in the early 1730s wanted to avoid the slave-based economy on which the other colonies were reliant. But Georgia's first settlers quickly yielded to the temptation of easy profits that slavery offered. By the time of the American Revolution, more than half of the people living in Georgia were slaves. Georgia became so committed to maintaining slavery that its delegates to the Continental Congress forced Thomas Jefferson to soften the language dealing with slavery in his initial draft of the Declaration of Independence in 1776.

For most of the eighteenth century, slaves were used on rice plantations in the state. During the Revolution, however, planters changed over to cotton, which was in high demand by the textile industry. The cotton gin, invented by Eli Whitney on a Savannah River plantation in 1793, made cotton Georgia's most important cash crop. Cotton plantations covered most the state by the 1830s. The banning of the African slave trade in 1808 had no discernible effect on slavery in Georgia. On the eve of the Civil War in 1860, slaves made up 44 percent of the state's population. Although slaveholders were prohibited by law from abusing or killing them, slaves were not allowed to provide evidence of their victimization in court. Most slaveholders employed a variety of physical punishments to keep their slaves in line, including the use of whips, boots, dogs, and wooden rods. The most effective means of keeping slaves obedient was the threat of selling them away from loved ones. Slaveholders also used threats of punishment to coerce female slaves into sleeping with them.

Throughout the antebellum era, slaves could be found both in the countryside and urban areas. Some thirty thousand slaves worked and lived in the Lowcountry, a 200-mile-long region stretching from Charleston, South Carolina, to St. Mary's Island, Georgia. Cholera epidemics frequently decimated the slave population in the Lowcountry within a matter of months. Infant mortality in the region was much higher than that experienced by white Americans at this time. Because the environment was so unhealthy, most slaveholders turned over supervision of the slaves to small groups of white overseers. Therefore, slaves living in the Lowcountry had more freedom than slaves who worked in the rice fields in Georgia, such as being allowed to return home as soon as their work was completed.

Slaves who worked in the cities also enjoyed a high degree of autonomy. In Savannah, for example, slaves were allowed to socialize in brothels and bars without supervision. Some black artisans who sold their wares in the marketplace were able to accumulate wealth. By contrast, slaves who labored in the cotton warehouses in Savannah were subjected to deplorable working conditions. Hundreds of slaves died from the summer heat and winter cold. On the whole, though, the slaves who worked in the rice fields suffered the most. On one Savannah rice plantation, 10 percent of the slave population perished in the fields between 1833 and 1861. Not surprisingly, the suffering of Georgia's slaves made a lasting imprint on the ghost lore of the state.

Undoubtedly, the majority of Georgia's ghost stories were produced during the Civil War. One of the most daring raids of the entire war, the Great Locomotive Chase, took place in Georgia. The second-bloodiest battle in the entire war, Chickamauga, was fought in Georgia. And the most notorious of all Civil War prison camps,

Andersonville, was located in Georgia. General Sherman's infamous March to the Sea brought the war to the home front and changed the face of warfare forever. During the Atlanta Campaign, massive armies clashed in what became the final turning point of the war. The fall of Fort Pulaski is noteworthy because it marked the first time rifled cannons were effectively used against brick and mortar fortifications. Nathan Bedford Forest defeated an entire invading force of cavalry mounted on mules in Rome, Georgia. The Massachusetts 54th, composed entirely of black soldiers, burned Darien. Wilson's Raiders, a huge Union force of 14,000 soldiers, fought what many experts believe to be the last battle of the Civil War in Columbus. An armed contingent of Georgia women called the Nancy Harts prevented Wilson's army from burning LaGrange. Confederate president Jefferson Davis was captured by the Union Army near Augusta. Georgia supplied the second-highest number of soldiers to the Southern cause—112,000. Thousands of these brave young men are buried in the cemeteries dotting the landscape. The exploits of the brave men and women who lived and died during the Civil War are celebrated in some of the state's most harrowing ghost stories.

Taylor gives one possible explanation for the appearances of ghosts who died as a result of piracy, slavery, or war, suggesting that sometimes strong emotions imprint themselves in a place where someone died, either accidentally or as the result of foul play. Occasionally these violent scenes are played out over and over again, like a film loop. Parapsychologists refer to this phenomenon as a residual haunting. This theory could explain why Captain Flint's death throes are still witnessed in the Pirate's House, why spectral soldiers reportedly wage war at Chickamauga Battlefield, or why echoes of the wailing voices of the drowned slaves at Ebo's Landing are still heard on St. Simons Island.

Some ghostly manifestations, however, have nothing to do with these monumental historic events. Folklorists have devised their own explanations for the return of these restless spirits. In *The Encyclopedia of Ghosts and Spirits,* Rosemary Ellen Guiley gives several reasons why sometimes the dead apparently come back. Some of the sightings included in this book follow Guiley's motifs. One of these motifs—that the ghost reappears to take care of unfinished business—may explain the little girl who seems still to be searching

Introduction

for her mother at Six Flags over Georgia. Some ghosts, according to Guiley, reenact their own deaths. A good example can be found in the Ezekiel Harris House, where the groans of the patriots who were hanged there reportedly are still heard by tourists. A number of ghost stories from Georgia suggest that some ghosts return to engage in the same activities they pursed when alive. These are the dutiful ghosts, like the vigilant sentries at Fort Pulaski. But the most fearsome spirits are those who return to punish the living. In Georgia's ghost lore, curses are used by vengeful spirits to vent their wrath through eternity. In Millidgeville, some believe that it was the curse pronounced on the town by Dixie Haygood, an epileptic with superhuman strength, that has turned the Yates family plot into a sinkhole.

Some of Georgia's most endearing ghost stories are those featuring ill-fated lovers. One might say that the unfinished business these spirits are trying to take care of is their unrequited or unconsummated love. A good example is the ghost of the young soldier who fell in love with Emily Galt, the daughter of the Confederate commandant of the arsenal at Augusta. Some students at Augusta State University say that the lovesick soldier is still searching the grounds for Emily. Many of the ill-fated lovers in Georgia's ghost stories committed suicide, such as Agnes Galloway of Brenau University, who hanged herself because the piano teacher she loved became engaged to a flapper. An even more famous example is Anna Powers, who was said to have jumped from the balcony of the 17Hundred90 Inn because her boyfriend went to sea and never returned. Suicide is considered by many Christians to be a mortal sin, and many believe these poor souls still walk the earth because they have been denied entrance into heaven.

In *Ghosts along the Cumberland*, Kentucky folklorist William Lynwood Montell says that sometimes ghosts return for no reason at all. Many of these ghosts are poltergeists, which Guiley defines as "a mischievous and sometimes malevolent spirit or energy that is characterized by noises, moving objects, and general physical disturbances." Some of these playful ghosts are the spirits of children, such as the little ghosts who roll billiard balls down the stairs of the Hamilton Turner Inn. Georgia's most famous poltergeist, the Surrency Ghost, reportedly threw a pair of irons at a minister's head and flung china ornaments on the floor.

Ghosts are not the only preternatural creatures believed to populate the psychic landscape of the state. In Georgia, some say, unseen beings push cars up hills. Prehistoric lizards cavort in the backwaters of the hill country. Werewolves stalk sheep—and human beings—in the light of the full moon. UFOs streak across the night sky and leave a lasting impression on a future president of the United States. Giant hogs hunt the hunters on a Georgia plantation. A doglike beast fuels the nightmares of Native Americans.

Clearly, peaches, peanuts, and pecans are not the only noteworthy products of this southern state that we think we know so well. Read on, and take a good look at its dark side. Chances are that Georgia will stay on your mind for a long time to come.

Augusta

AUGUSTA IS THE SECOND-OLDEST AND SECOND-LARGEST CITY IN Georgia. Named in honor of the mother of King George III, Augusta's spiritual roots extend all the way back to the mid-eighteenth century. Fifteen years after Augusta's founding in 1735, St. Paul's Church was built to meet the needs of the increasing numbers of settlers in the area. Years later, Augusta became the birthplace of the Southern Baptist denomination, as well as the site of the nation's oldest autonomous African-American Baptist church.

But Augusta's religious history is not the only reason why it is a spiritual city. Ghosts seem to abound in Augusta, likely due in large part to its violent past. During the Revolutionary War, when Augusta became the new state capital, it was captured twice by the British. Even though General William T. Sherman did not burn Augusta in 1864, the city suffered mightily during the Civil War. Two thousand of the soldiers trained at the arsenal were sent into active duty; hundreds of these young men never returned. And Augusta's tragic legacy of slavery generated one of the city's most gruesome ghost legends: the story of the Resurrection Man.

The Grisly Secret of the Old Medical College

The Medical Academy of Georgia opened on October 1, 1829, in Augusta. The college went through several name changes before settling on the Medical College of Georgia in 1833. The institution's first academic building, the Old Medical College, was constructed between 1834 and 1835 by architect Charles Blaney Cluskey at a cost of $14,567. The Old Medical College exemplifies the Greek Revival style, with its Doric portico and central rotunda. Classes were taught in the Old Medical College from 1834 to 1913, when the college moved to a larger building. The Old Medical College was used by the Academy of Richmond County for training and teaching until 1926. Later, the building was leased by the Garden Club of Augusta. It also housed the Augusta Genealogical Society. In 1989, when the Medical College of Georgia Foundation began restoring the old building, workers made a gruesome discovery in the basement that lent validity to the campus legend of a mysterious figure called the Resurrection Man.

The Resurrection Man was a nickname doctors gave to a slave named Grandison Harris. The Medical College bought the thirty-six-year-old Gullah slave off an auction block in Charleston, South Carolina, for $700. His new owners broke the law by teaching him to read and write. They also had him sit in on anatomy classes. Their goal was to transform Grandison into a first-rate grave robber. Dissection was illegal in Georgia until 1887, so medical schools procured their cadavers from unscrupulous men who dug up recently interred corpses in graveyard.

Like most grave robbers, Grandison kept abreast of burials by reading the obituary column in the newspaper. Then, under cover of darkness, he sneaked into the largest black graveyard in Augusta, Cedar Grove Cemetery. Before he started digging, Grandison memorized the placement of the flowers and grave marker so that he could replace them exactly the way they were originally. In an interview conducted in 1938, Eugene Murphy, a professor at the Medical College of Georgia, said that Grandison usually smashed the upper end of the coffin with an ax and pulled the dead body out of the grave. Grandison was so skilled at his work that it was almost impossible to tell that the contents of the grave were stolen.

After the Civil War, Grandison left the Medical College briefly but then returned as the school "porter," or janitor. His unofficial role, however, was the same as before: Medical College grave robber. Rumors of Grandison's nocturnal activities were finally confirmed in 1889. Members of Augusta's black community were so upset that the city narrowly avoided a riot. Understandably, they were horrified by the thought that their loved ones might have been exhumed and dissected. But Grandison miraculously escaped retribution from the relatives of the corpses he had stolen. He died in 1911 at age ninety-five. Ironically, he was buried in the same cemetery that he had pillaged for more than half a century, Cedar Grove Cemetery.

Grandison Harris remained a shadowy historical footnote until the proof of his handiwork was uncovered in the basement of the Old Medical College. Stephanie Hunter, writing for the *Augusta Chronicle* online, says that workers discovered the remains of four thousand cadavers in the basement. Grandison apparently believed that the best way to dispose of the dissected corpses was to bury them in the basement's earthen floor. An article published in the spring 1995 edition of the *Newsletter of the African-American Archaeology Network* reported that a team of archaeologists recovered hundreds of cadaver parts during the excavation of the basement. Some of the bones had specimen numbers written on them with india ink. Evidence indicated that the Medical College of Georgia's professors preferred as cadavers African Americans over Euro-Americans, adults over children, and males over females. A foul-smelling vat that held organs and body parts preserved in whiskey was also found in the basement. After the bones were subjected to intensive study, they were reinterred in Grove Hill Cemetery in 1998, not far from the grave of the man who had "resurrected" them.

Even though all of the players in this tragic period in the college's history are dead and buried, some of them might not be entirely at rest. In recent years, construction workers and employees have heard groaning sounds on the third floor of the Old Medical College late at night. The sources of the eerie noises have never been found. Some people believe that renovations have disturbed the spirits of the people whose graves Grandison Harris robbed. In recent years, there have been reports of Grandison Harris's ghost walking along the headstones in Cedar Grove Cemetery, possibly ruminating over the heartache his grave robbing brought to his own people.

Ghostly Patriots at the Ezekiel Harris House

The Ezekiel Harris House, the second-oldest house in Augusta, is a relic of the days of tobacco farms and slavery. Ezekiel Harris came to Georgia from Edgefield, South Carolina, in the waning years of the eighteenth century, with the intention of founding a town that would some day rival Augusta. This town, which he planned to call Harrisburg, would grow up around a tobacco warehouse and inspection station. In 1797, he began construction on a three-story inn where tobacco planters would receive free accommodations during their stay in Harrisburg.

The inn, now known as the Ezekiel Harris House, has also been known as the White House and the MacKay House. It is remembered today as the site of a fierce battle that raged between British and American forces during the Revolutionary War in 1780. Because the Ezekiel Harris House was not built until after the Revolutionary War, the White House or MacKay House was probably an entirely different building. Indeed, evidence discovered in 1975 indicates that the White House or MacKay House actually stood across the street from the Ezekiel Harris House. Many residents of Augusta believe that ghosts from a tragic act of injustice are now residing in the old building.

In September 1780, Colonel Thomas Brown, along with a group of loyalists and Cherokee Indians, was holed up inside the MacKay Trading Post. General Elijah Clarke and his army of three hundred patriots decided to engage the British forces who had burned their farms and slaughtered their cows. Following a fierce exchange of gunfire, the loyalists dug in around the trading post while waiting for the next assault. With no food or water readily available, Brown's men subsisted on urine and seasoned pumpkins. Just when it seemed as if the loyalists could hold out no longer, a British colonel named Cruger arrived with more men and munitions. Bolstered by the new additions to his forces, Brown's men routed Clarke's forces and emerged victorious. After Clarke's retreat, Brown decided to punish the twenty-nine patriots who had been left behind. According to the legend, Brown hanged thirteen of the patriots and turned over the remaining sixteen to the Cherokees to be tortured. Years later, Brown denied that this incident ever occurred.

In the absence of the McKay Trading Post, which was destroyed in battle in 1781, the unquiet spirits of the twenty-nine patriots apparently have been making their presence known in the Ezekiel Harris House. For generations, people walking up the stairs have claimed that when they stop on the thirteenth step, they can hear the groans of the executed patriots. Others say they have heard the creaking of swinging ropes, straining from the weight of dead patriots, inside the house. The only actual sighting is that of a woman, supposedly the ghost of the mother of two brothers who were hanged by Colonel Brown. Dressed in a white gown and holding a white handkerchief, the sad, lonely figure passes through the rooms on the third floor, searching for her lost sons. Ghost stories like the ones generated around the Ezekiel Harris House are still told because of the messages they convey regarding the true cost of war, both in battle and on the home front.

The Haunted Pillar

Without a doubt, Augusta's best-known ghost story is based around a very unusual landmark in the middle of town. In 1829, the story goes, a preacher was trying to make himself heard amid the hustle and bustle of the Lower Market, where people had come to buy fruit, vegetables, and livestock. One version of the story has it that a policeman asked him to stop preaching because he was disturbing the shoppers. In another version, the preacher became frustrated because the people were paying more attention to their material needs than to their spiritual needs. At any rate, the preacher cursed the city of Augusta. He foretold of a great wind that would sweep away the marketplace. Only a single stone pillar would be spared. The preacher added that anyone who touched or tried to move the pillar would die.

On February 8, 1878, the preacher's prophecy came true. A freakish winter tornado leveled the Lower Market; only a single pillar was left standing. Soon afterward, a writer for the *Augusta Chronicle* suggested that a new market should never be built on the same location because "it was, at best, an unsightly edifice and marred the grand boulevard upon which it was mistakenly located."

The ill-advised attempts of people to defy the preacher's warning regarding the pillar has been the stuff of legend in Augusta for

over a century. According to one tale, one of the people who were clearing the debris left by the tornado in 1878 wanted to impress the crowd by tying ropes to the pillar and attempting to pull it down. He had no sooner finished fastening the ropes to the pillar than he dropped dead of a heart attack. Another legend has it that a grocer who had purchased the pillar for $50 moved it to Fifth and Broad Streets. He died shortly after that. A few years later, during construction on Broad Street, two more men tried to pull the pillar down with ropes, only to be struck by lightning. Visitors who tried to take away fragments of the pillar became ill and were forced to extend their stay in Augusta. Not long ago, a man driving along Broad Street accidentally hit the pillar. Though the car was barely damaged, the driver died at the scene.

The truth is, however, not everyone who has come into contact with the pillar has died. In 1935, the *Augusta Chronicle* reported that a car ran into the pillar "and reduced it to a pile of brick and cement," but the driver escaped injury. The pillar was rebuilt by a local market owner. In 1936, the column was moved to the southwest corner of Fifth and Broad Streets, but none of the workmen suffered any ill effects whatsoever. On Friday, June 13, 1958—certainly not a good day to tempt a curse—a bale of cotton on a passing truck bumped into the column and knocked it over. Once again, the driver was not injured. Following this incident, the pillar was moved eight feet from the curb to prevent future accidents.

The Vain Ghost in the Benet House

Augusta State College has two faces. Although the academic face predominates today, vestiges of its military past still remain. In 1793, President George Washington established an arsenal near the river. Black fever made the arsenal unlivable, so it was moved across the river in 1826. The original barracks, jail, and headquarters building still remain and have been converted for academic purposes. The commandant's house is now the president's home. In 1911, Stephen Vincent Benét, who was born in 1898, began his writing career here after moving to Augusta in 1911. Benét, who wrote poetry and short stories, won a Pulitzer Prize in 1928 for his Civil War poem *John Brown's Body* but is best known today for the short stories "I Remember Babylon" and "The Devil and Daniel

Webster." Benét is gone now, having died in 1943. But legends about an earlier occupant of the house still remain.

In *Haunted Augusta and Local Legends,* Sean Joiner recounts the tale of a commander who lived with his beautiful wife in the house in the nineteenth century. She was a vain woman whose wardrobe was among the finest in Augusta. Every morning, her maid brought her a cup of tea, which she drank while admiring herself in the mirror. One morning, the maid entered her mistress's room and was horrified to find the woman lying on the floor dead. Her husband told authorities that he had brought her a cup of tea before going hunting just before dawn. He was never formally accused of the crime, although suspicions of his guilt hounded him for the rest of his life. Today the clothes in her closet have been seen swaying back and forth, as if an invisible hand is searching for just the right look for the evening.

According to another legend, the man who commanded the arsenal during Reconstruction hired his nephew to work for him for $2 an hour. The commander's preferential treatment of the young man instilled jealousy in the other workers, who received much less pay for the same work. One day the commander's nephew left work to get a piece of pie; he was shot and killed on the steps of the house. It seems that his appetite for pie has never been satisfied. People occasionally hear noises coming from the kitchen. They say the young man is still searching the cabinets for a piece of pie.

Over the years, students and employees have experienced phenomena that cannot be attributed to a specific spirit. People have heard the sounds of a rocking chair, footsteps upstairs, and doors slamming. Strange images have been seen in mirrors. One wonders when Stephen Vincent Benét might make an appearance, if he hasn't already.

The Tragic Lovers of Bellevue Hall

Many colleges and universities in Georgia have some sort of connection to the Civil War, but only Augusta State University was actually built on the site of an arsenal. The U.S. Arsenal was originally located on the banks of the Savannah River. Frequent outbreaks of fever among the ranks forced the military to move the arsenal to a hill location on seventy-two acres of land owned by

Senator Freeman Walker in 1826. Walker sold his Sands Hill cottage, called Bellevue, for $6,000. A small plot of land was set aside for the Walker family cemetery.

By 1828, four buildings connected by a loopholed wall were constructed. That same year, the arsenal began supplying arms for the Harpers Ferry Armory and the Georgia militia. Troops stationed there fought in the Seminole War in 1835 as well as in campaigns against the Creek Indians. During the Civil War, thirty companies of soldiers from the Augusta area were trained at the arsenal. In May 1865, the arsenal was once again taken over by the U.S. government. Decades later, in 1958, Augusta College was created on the same tract of land where soldiers were once trained for combat. Legend has it that one of these soldiers is responsible for the haunting of Bellevue Hall.

In 1861, Bellevue Hall was owned by John Galt. One of his two daughters, Emily, fell in love with one of the young soldiers at the armory. The couple became engaged and planned to marry after the young man returned from the war. Emily sported a huge diamond engagement ring, which she used to etch her name into a window in one of the rooms on the second floor. Her sister Lucy then took the ring and scratched her name alongside of Emily's. Emily begged her fiancé not to go to war, but after several heated arguments, he kissed her good-bye and went off to join the Confederate forces. Not long afterward, her lover was killed in action. Tortured by the thought that her dreams of marital bliss would never come true, Emily threw herself out the same second-story window where she had etched her name and fell to her death.

Bellevue Hall now houses several campus offices. Several employees at the Counseling and Testing Center have reported hearing raised voices coming from the hallway after everyone else has left for the day. On other occasions, televisions and telephones in the building have malfunctioned temporarily for no apparent reason. It seems that Emily Galt is still venting her anger at being left while her lover marched off to his death. The ghost of Emily's young soldier has also been seen roaming the campus in search of his lost love.

Haunted Rains Hall

Rains Hall hearkens back to the days when a federal arsenal was located on the present-day site of Augusta State University. Rains Hall is one of four military buildings constructed between 1828 and 1829. The two-story, white-columned building, which was home to the second in command of the arsenal, was named in honor of Confederate Colonel George Washington Rains, who was regent of Augusta State's parent institution, the Academy of Richmond County. Today the offices of the university president and Public Relations and Publications are housed in the old building. According to the women who work in public relations, Rains Hall might be home to something else as well.

In an interview with Kimberly Lawson for *Augusta* magazine, university director of public relations Kathy Schofe said she has had several unsettling experiences since taking her present position in 1997. One evening, she and the former director were working late when they heard several doorknobs shake in the hallway. At first they assumed that security was just making sure all the offices were locked. The two women had left their office and were halfway down the stairs when they heard the sound of muffled voices coming from the basement. Schofe said it sounded as if the volume of a radio had been turned way down. This time they realized they had encountered something highly unusual. Schofe called security and asked to be accompanied to her car.

Kim Smith, who also works in public relations, had her own weird experience. She was working by herself one day when she heard a strange noise coming from the hallway. She walked out of her office into the hallway and was shocked to see the blinds in the windows moving by themselves. It looked as if an invisible hand were running up and down the blinds. She was certain that no breeze was blowing through the building at the time.

The identity of the ghost has never been discovered, but a public safety officer and a custodian reported seeing a Confederate officer standing on the stairway in Rains Hall. The employees at Rains Hall might agree that buildings are not the only remnants of the past that can be found on the campus of Augusta State University.

Boykin Wright Hall's Vigilant Judge

Built in 1900, Boykin Wright Hall was originally the home of the former Georgia supreme court justice. It is located, appropriately, just across from the cemeteries. The two-story house was given to Augusta State University by Boykin Wright's daughter, Marguerite Wright Hillman. Some employees believe that the Justice never completely turned over his beautiful home to be used by an administrator.

Writing in *Augusta* magazine, Kimberly Lawson says that Cyndi White, former administrative assistant to the dean of students, and Gina Thurman, the current vice president of student services, were working in the building when they heard a loud noise coming from upstairs. Cyndi said it sounded as if a large adult had collapsed and rolled a couple times on the floor. Concerned that someone had fainted or had an accident, the two women rushed up the stairs. Expecting to find a prostrate figure writhing in pain on the floor, they were surprised to discover that nothing was out of order, with the exception of a plastic picture frame that was lying on the floor.

The next Monday, a student assistant leaving Cyndi's office was about to tell her that she would come back soon when a look of terror swept across her face. She instinctively sensed that some unearthly presence was standing behind her. Cyndi and Gina, who had been facing the girl, saw the reason why the girl had become so frightened: A shadowy, manlike shape had suddenly appeared at the door and just as quickly dematerialized.

The ghost, who is called Boykin, is reputed to be responsible for another strange occurrence inside the Justice's former home. One of the rooms in the building had been locked for many years, and most people assumed that the key had been lost. Eager to see what was inside, Cyndi had the door removed from its hinges. She and the workmen were puzzled by what they found: the door had been dead-bolted from the inside. Apparently, Boykin values his privacy.

The Nosy Ghost of Rosemary Hall

James Urquhart Jackson became a visionary at an early age. The story goes that as a boy, he gazed across the Savannah River—which separates Augusta from South Carolina—and asked his father why no one had developed those beautiful hills. Jackson acted upon that dream soon after graduating from the University of Georgia. After starting a successful brokerage firm, he began making plans for creating a new city, complete with streets, lights, and water. After a steel bridge was built spanning the Savannah River from Thirteenth Street in Augusta in 1891, Jackson started a trolley line connecting Augusta and his new city, North Augusta, South Carolina, in 1897.

Jackson went on to found several North Augusta companies, including the North Augusta Water and Gas Company and the Augusta-Aiken Railway. His proudest, and most disappointing, accomplishment was the construction of the Hampton Terrace Hotel in 1902, which attracted such captains of industry as John D. Rockefeller, Marshall Field, and Harvey Firestone. The hotel burned to the ground in 1916. That same year, Jackson built a home at the corner of Carolina and Forrest Avenues for his family with his second wife, Edith Barrington King. Rosemary Hall, as his house became known, exists as a testament to Jackson's wealth and power, as well as evidence that there might be life after death.

Rosemary Hall remained in the Jackson family until 1983, when it was purchased by Bill and Millie Thompson, who did extensive renovations on the home. It was then sold to a group of Japanese investors, who turned it into a bed-and-breakfast. The present owners of Rosemary Hall have complemented all twenty rooms and six suites with period antiques, custom-made carpets, and fine art. Rosemary Hall's appeal is enhanced by its fifty-foot-high columns, a magnificent English staircase, and over seventy camellia bushes, many of which were planted more than seventy-five years ago.

Some people believe that the current owners' preservation efforts have attracted the attention of Jackson's second wife, Edith Barrington King. Ever since the bed-and-breakfast opened its doors, guests have reported seeing a short, elderly woman walking up the main stairs leading to the second floor. Sean Joiner, author of *Haunted Augusta,* says that the old lady has been seen walking on the second floor of the hotel as well. She is also said to peek in on guests as they are sleeping in their rooms. Jackson's wife has been credited with moving objects from one room to another. Even though Edith is clearly a supernatural presence, eyewitnesses are usually filled not with a sense of dread, but a feeling of peace.

Bones in the Garden

The Federal Style House at Fifth and Greene Streets was built by Gabriel Manigault for Nicholas Ware in 1818. Because construction costs totaled $40,000, an extravagant sum at that time, the four-level house was dubbed Ware's Folly. Ware, who became mayor of Augusta and served in the Georgia legislature, entertained a number of dignitaries in his home, including the Marquis de Lafayette. Lafayette attended a ball in the home in 1825. A number of Augusta's most prominent families lived—and died—in the house throughout the nineteenth and twentieth centuries. In fact, one of the original windows in the house still bears the etching of the initials of a previous owner from the 1880s. Now the home of the Gertrude Herbert Institute of Art, it is a center for art classes and traveling art shows. The Nicholas Ware House may also be the center of paranormal activity.

Joiner, in *Haunted Augusta,* says that no apparitions have been seen by any of the owners of the house. Some people, however, have heard strange noises in the house. Others have felt that they were living with a friendly spirit. The disturbances might be connected to a grisly discovery made in 1935, when workmen hired to renovate the house found some bones inside a wall on the first floor. The bones were assumed to be those of an animal—until a young woman told of something that had happened to her as a child. One day, she was digging around in the flower garden, even though her mother had repeatedly told her not to. She dug up what appeared at first to be several oddly shaped white rocks. When she picked them up, however, she realized that the light, porous objects were actually bones. She ran into the house and up the stairs to the attic, searching for a place to hide the bones. Suddenly she heard her mother enter the house. Concerned that her mother would see the bones and realize her daughter had dug in the garden against her orders, she dropped the bones down a hole in the attic. The bones lodged behind the wall in the first floor and remained there until they were found by the workmen. To this day, no one knows whose bones were buried in the garden. Perhaps the owner of the bones prefers the house over the garden.

The Phantom of Sibley Mill

Augusta became an industrial center in large part because of its canal, which was built between 1845 and 1847. During the Civil War, the most important of these industries was the Confederate Powder Works. Until the factory ceased operations on April 18, 1865, it produced 2,750,000 pounds of gunpowder. In 1872, the Powder Works buildings were sold to investors and torn down, with the exception of the 153-foot obelisk chimney, which was left standing as a monument to the Confederate dead.

After the Augusta Canal was expanded between 1872 and 1875, plans were made for a cotton mill. In 1880, the John P. King and Sibley Cotton Mills were built on the site of the Powder Works with bricks salvaged from the dismantled buildings. They were designed after the Powder Works and England's House of Parliament. Today the Sibley Mill is one of only two late-nineteenth-century textile mills still operating along the Augusta Canal. Owned and operated by the Avondale Corporation, the old mill is now a denim finishing plant. Aside from making thousands of feet of cloth, the Sibley Mill has also produced a chilling ghost story.

In the early 1900s, women worked alongside men on the weaving machines. One of these women was Maude Williams, who was secretly having an affair with a married man named Arthur Glover. On October 20, 1906, Glover barged into the mill and shot Maude with a pistol. Later Glover confessed that he was distraught because Maude had broken up with him the day before. Joiner says in *Haunted Augusta* that not long after the murder, workers reported seeing the ghost of Maude Williams walking past the weaving machine when the room was supposed to be empty. New employees who attempted to speak to the woman were baffled when she went on her way without even acknowledging their presence. Every time Maude Williams's ghost has been seen, the weaving machine was operating at a time when it should have been turned off. Maude's ghost has not been seen in the Sibley Mill for many years, possibly because she has finally decided that it is time to retire.

Central Georgia

FOR THE MOST PART, CENTRAL GEORGIA LIES WITHIN THE SOUTHERN boundary of the piedmont land region. Known for its gently rolling hills, this region gradually slopes down toward the south. Some of the area's largest cities, such as Columbus and Macon, were founded at water-power sites, where rivers flow from the piedmont to the coastal plains and form falls and rapids. People have raised cotton, fruit, vegetables, and sweet potatoes in this region for generations.

Scores of rich cotton planters lived and flourished in Central Georgia. These men flaunted their wealth by building large, ostentatious Greek Revival mansions. As patrons of the arts, they were avid supporters of venues such as the Springer Opera House in Columbus. The lives of luxury these people enjoyed stand in stark contrast to the deplorable living conditions endured by the prisoners at Andersonville, one of the region's most haunted sites.

Andersonville's Imprisoned Spirits

Atrocities were committed at all prisons, Confederate and Federal, during the Civil War, but Andersonville Prison is probably the most notorious. Selected because of the availability of fresh water and its proximity to the Southwestern Railroad, the original site of Andersonville Prison encompassed 16.5 acres and was designed to hold

ten thousand Union prisoners. The walls of the stockade were constructed of pine logs and were 1,010 feet long and 1,780 feet wide.
Prisoners who walked through the "dead line," a light fence erected
nineteen feet inside the stockade, were shot by sentries. The
designer of the prison, Captain W. Sidney Winder, believed that
Andersonville's abundance of fresh air and pure water would make
the facility much more humane than the conventional prisons and
dungeons of the time.

But Winder's idealism soon proved to be ill founded. The first
trainload of prisoners arrived in February 1864; by June, the prison
population had ballooned to twenty thousand. Ghastly living conditions immediately followed. Sweetwater, the ironically named
stream running through the middle of the camp, soon became a
foul sewer. The planned barracks were never built. Prisoners huddled in tents and log shelters, seeking protection from the summer
sun and winter chill. Patches of marsh rendered 85 percent of the
land uninhabitable, making living conditions even more cramped.
Rations were vermin-infested and moldy. Prisoners by the score
died of starvation, infection, exposure, and disease, especially
scurvy, diarrhea, and dysentery. By the end of the war, thirteen
thousand prisoners had died in the man-made hellhole. Some people say that psychic energy released by the people who suffered
and died so tragically at Andersonville has been absorbed by every
corner of present day Andersonville National Historic Site.

The names of most of the restless spirits of Andersonville are
unknown, but a few of the prison's ghosts have been tentatively
identified. One of these spirits is that of a man dressed in black,
holding an umbrella. The detailed description of the phantom given
by eyewitnesses such as Robert Berry has led park officials to spec-
ulate that the ghost could be the spirit of Father Whelan, a priest
who paid daily visits to the sick and dying in the prison toward the
end of the war. Prisoners released from Andersonville recalled that
Father Whelan often carried an umbrella to protect himself from
the merciless sun.

Authorities have had more difficulty identifying the apparition
witnessed by three women who were returning one night from a
civic meeting in Americus. They had no sooner passed the road
marker for Andersonville Prison when they saw a man standing
beside the road in a military uniform. The women immediately

turned the car around and returned to the place where they had seen the soldier, but he was gone. A history buff convinced the women that they had seen the ghost of Major Henry Wirz, the Swiss commandant of Andersonville Prison, who was tried, convicted, and hanged as a war criminal. Because Wirz was put in command of the camp late in the war and was not responsible for the deplorable conditions in the prison, many people believe that his restless spirit is still seeking vindication.

The most commonly reported ghosts in the historic site are the infamous Raiders of Andersonville. The Raiders were a loose-knit group of five hundred thugs who ruled the prison during most of its existence. Under the leadership of a scoundrel named Willie Collins, the Raiders stole money, food, and clothing from men who were too weak or ill to defend themselves. When Wirz learned of the Raiders from a guard, he permitted the prisoners to try their assailants. As a result of the trials, six of the Raiders were hanged on July 11, 1864, including Collins. The ghosts of the six executed Raiders are usually blamed for most of the strange occurrences at the park, including an incident reported in *Blue and Gray Magazine Guide to Haunted Places of the Civil War.* One day, two tourists who had heard the tour guides tell the story of the Raiders of Andersonville Prison became so outraged that one of them cursed the Raiders and spit on Collins's grave. That night, while the two young men were camping out at a site near Americus, they were awakened by the sound of footsteps on the drive leading to the campsite. They investigated the small area around their sleeping bags and even shouted at the intruders to stop, but the tramping sound continued, coming closer and closer. Finally the two young men became so unnerved that they broke camp in the middle of the night. They learned a hard lesson that night: that all spirits demand respect, even those who do not deserve it.

The Show Still Goes on in the Springer Opera House

No one living in Columbus in the 1850s could have imagined that an immigrant grocer from Alsace who had just arrived in the United States would go on to build one of the most spectacular opera houses in the entire Southeast. Aside from his business acumen, which would make him a fortune, Francis Joseph Springer brought with him from northern Europe his love of the arts. Springer even demolished his grocery store so that his opera house could be built on one of the busiest corners in the city.

The Springer Opera House opened on February 21, 1871, with a concert presented by members of the Trinity Episcopal Church. For the next half century, luminaries such as Franklin Delano Roosevelt, General Tom Thumb, Oscar Wilde, Will Rogers, Booker T. Washington, Ethel Barrymore, William Jennings Bryan, and Irving Berlin appeared at the Springer.

The Springer Opera House prospered until the stock market crash of 1929. Road companies that provided the lifeblood of American theater went out of business, so the owners of the Springer were forced by financial necessity to convert it into a movie theater in the 1940s. The eventual decline of Columbus's historic district hastened the Springer's demise.

In 1964, the old brick theater was rescued from the wrecking ball at the last minute by Emily Woodruff Hall and other concerned citizens who raised the money to restore the Springer to its former glory. After some essential repairs were made, the opera house reopened in 1965. In 1998-99, the state completely renovated the Springer Opera House at the cost of $12 million. Not only does history come alive in the Springer, but it seems that one of American theater's greatest nineteenth-century actors does as well.

The Springer Opera House had been open for five years when Edwin Booth arrived in Columbus to play Hamlet. He had chosen this play to restore his reputation in 1866, a year after his brother, John Wilkes Booth, had assassinated Abraham Lincoln. Soon audiences throughout the land packed theaters to see America's greatest actor perform in his greatest role. At the end of Booth's performance in Columbus, he was delighted by the thunderous applause he received—so much so that, according to some people, he never really left the Springer.

Edwin Booth's spirit has been blamed for poltergeist activity in the opera house. Chris Wangler reports in *Ghost Stories of Georgia* that one morning, several pairs of shoes from the prop room were discovered lined up at the top of a stairway. One employee witnessed a cowboy hat vanish into a wall. Stage lights have mysteriously blinked on and off. Workers have often heard strange, soothing music filling the theater and recall Edwin's habit of playing music to calm down his father, Junius Brutus Booth, during his bouts of madness.

The most widely circulated ghost story concerns a theater official who was checking on some costumes one evening in the early 1970s. She was dismayed to discover that the key to the heavy metal door sealing off the costume wing was not in the desk in the office, where it was supposed to be. She walked upstairs to see if someone had left the key in the lock, but it was nowhere to be found. When she returned to the office, she found the key lying on the desk. Exasperated, she trudged up the stairs once more to the costume wing. To her surprise, she discovered that the padlock was unlocked, the hasp gently swaying back and forth.

In 2004, a paranormal group from Loganville called the Foundation for Paranormal Research conducted a twenty-four-hour investigation at the Springer Opera House. They were accompanied by a camera crew from local television station WTVM. Afterward, Rick Heflin, the director of the group, revealed their findings: "We got orbs [ghostly ball of light], we got EVPs [electronic voice phenomena], we got a picture of a seat that was glowing like it was on fire." Like hundreds of people who viewed the television footage of the investigation, Heflin is convinced that some disembodied spirit— perhaps the ghost of Edwin Booth—is still making its presence known at the Springer Opera House.

The Haunting of Hay House

When wealthy investor William Butler Johnston set about building his home in 1855, he was very much aware that one of the benefits of being a millionaire was the freedom to live any way he wished. Johnston opted for the Italian Renaissance Revival style, which is characterized by curves and arches instead of the straight lines of the Greek Revival style favored by many rich southerners at that time. He furnished his eighteen-thousand-square-foot, twenty-four-room mansion with state-of-the-art amenities: central heat, an in-house kitchen, a speaker system, hot and cold running water, and an elaborate ventilation system. Johnston and his wife, the former Anne Clark Tracy, filled their home with sculptures, paintings, and porcelains that they had purchased on their extended honeymoon in Europe in 1851. After construction was completed in 1859, Johnston's mansion became known as the Palace of the South. The couple even set aside an entire room for their most important piece, an 1857 marble statue called *Ruth Gleaning,* by American expatriate sculptor Randolph Rogers.

But even a home as magnificent as the Johnstons' could not insulate William and Anne from tragedy. Their first four children died very young. Until her fifth child, Caroline, was born July 1862, Anne was too grief-stricken to leave her bed most of the time. During the Civil War, General Sherman bypassed Macon, but three weeks after the war ended, General James H. Wilson fired his cannons at the cupola of the Johnstons' mansion, leaving two huge craters that were not filled until the early 1990s. The house remained in the Johnston family until the sixth child, Mary Ellen, and her husband, William H. Felton, took over the residence in 1896. In 1926, the house passed out of the hands of the Johnston family entirely when Parks Lee Hay, founder of the Bankers' Health and Life Insurance Company, became the next owner. Since 1977, the Johnston-Felton-Hay House has been owned and operated as a museum by the Georgia Trust for Historic Preservation. Thanks to the efforts of the caretakers and the museum staff, the past is still alive at the old mansion—maybe, according to some people, in a very unsettling way.

Most of the paranormal activity that has been witnessed inside the Hay House has occurred after 1980, when the old mansion was extensively renovated. Many workmen and staff members who reported seeing the ghosts of two females, two men, and a small child during this period have accepted the theory that when structural changes are made in an old building, dormant ghosts "wake up" and become active. In *Banshees, Bugles and Belles,* Barbara Duffey reports that a former director of the Hay House, Fran La Farge, said she saw the figure of a woman with braided hair standing in the hallway. She immediately recognized the woman as the ghost of Anne Tracy Johnston from the portraits and pictures hanging in the house. On another occasion, the director was in the dining room all by herself late one night when she felt a blast of hot air. She was so taken aback by the sudden change in temperature that she was totally unprepared for the blast of cold air that followed. She did not really believe in ghosts, however, until the unexplained footsteps she heard climbing the stairs to the second floor set off the security alarm.

Chester Davis, who served as the houseman and tour guide at the Hay House, did not talk about the bizarre events he had witnessed until other people began telling their stories. In an interview published in the *Macon Telegraph and News* in 1984, Davis told the reporter that he had seen three ghosts after 1980. One day, he was polishing the silver doorknobs when he saw a gentleman about fifty-five years of age standing in the dining room. The man was wearing blue pants and a white shirt. Davis's description matched that of Judge William H. Felton, William Johnston's son-in-law. Davis's second sighting occurred at noon one day when a lady in her sixties wearing a white checked dress and a straw hat suddenly appeared at the front door. As she began to reach for the doorbell, she vanished. The next day, as Davis was polishing the hinges on the front door, he saw a woman around thirty years old in a purple dress standing on the front lawn by the driveway. When he took a second glance at her, she disappeared. Staff members believe her to be the spirit of Luisa McGill Gibson, the wife of William Felton Jr. The staff has changed since La Farge and Davis had their experiences in the Hay House, but many residents of Macon believe that the ghosts are still there.

The Traveling Ghost of the Colonel George W. Fish House

When Colonel George W. Fish arrived in Oglethorpe from Pulaski County in 1852, he envisioned building a home on Randolph Street unlike any other house in the area. His house, modeled after those of wealthy British planters in the West Indies, was a two-story structure with two banistered flights of steps rising from the front to the second-floor portico. He and his wife planted camellia bushes imported from France on the spacious grounds. Colonel Fish, also known as Judge Fish, was a prominent attorney who spent much of his time in the courthouse in Oglethorpe. In 1871, the courthouse, which was the focus of much of Fish's life, also became the scene of his death.

One spring night, Colonel Fish had just returned to the courthouse from a business trip in Macon. Hiding in the shadows was John Holsenback, whom the Colonel had offended somehow. Holsenback's accomplice was Jim Lloyd, who encouraged his friend to kill Fish because the Colonel was paying too much attention to Lloyd's wife. As soon as Colonel Fish was in range, Holsenback fired, mortally wounding him. Ironically, Holsenback used Fish's own gun, which he had dropped off at the local gun shop to be repaired. In the confusion following the murder, Holsenback melted into the crowd. To avoid suspicion, he helped return the Colonel's body to the Fish home and also helped place the corpse into the coffin.

After the Colonel's funeral, Governor Rufus sent two detectives named Rasberry and Murphy to investigate the murder. One day, Murphy followed Holsenback into a shop. He picked up a woven fish basket, peered through it, and accused Holsenback of murdering Fish. Holsenback was so unnerved that he confessed; he also implicated his friend, Jim Lloyd. Both men were arrested and taken to the county jail. In order to collect more information against the duo, the two detectives hid inside a large box, which was disguised as a washstand, and listened in on their conversation. As soon as the detectives believed they had heard enough, they emerged from their hiding place and confronted the two prisoners. The detectives' testimony helped convict Holsenback and Lloyd, who were hanged in June 1871.

M. L. Shealy bought the house from Colonel Fish's widow in 1872. In 1962, Mr. and Mrs. Donald Nelson became the third family to occupy the Fish House. The Nelsons initially ignored the stories told by the Shealys' former servants about the sounds of raised voices and footsteps downstairs when no one else was around. But strange things began to happen in 1969, when the Nelsons undertook the Herculean task of moving the Fish House from Oglethorpe to Americus. The carpenters who prepared the foundations for the house in Americus had to work at night. Before long, someone—or something—began interfering with their progress. The next day, workmen would find that piles of sand were strewn about, mortar boxes were overturned, and tools were missing. Before the house was ready to move, two crews walked off the job site, convinced that something supernatural was hindering them. Just before the house was moved, a photograph Mr. Nelson took of it showed a blurry white mass. During the move, the house slid off the rig that was hauling it and fell into a ditch for no apparent reason.

Nelson said he became acquainted with the ghost soon after the house was placed on its foundations in Americus. In a story reported in the August 5, 1973, edition of the *Macon Telegraph and News*, Nelson said that he was sleeping in his chair in front of his fireplace when a lean, dark-haired man in Victorian clothing suddenly materialized directly in front of him. The ghost told Nelson that he was not happy that his house had been moved to Americus, but he was pleased with the restoration work that had been done and was at peace. Nelson was relieved to learn that he and his family would not be living with an angry spirit.

The house changed hands again in 1971, when it was purchased by Dr. and Mrs. Gatewood Dudley, who had returned to Americus after serving three years at the Air Force Hospital in London. In an interview in the April 29, 1973, issue of the *Atlanta Journal and Constitution* magazine, Dr. Dudley said that the ghost totally ignored the rooms to the left of the hall. He preferred the large dining room on the right side, possibly because at that time, that part of the house had not been wired for electricity and was illuminated by candlelight. Dudley said that his children were particularly afraid of the portrait of William Harris Crawford hanging in the dining room. One of his daughters, Shannon, always ran through the dining room, because she felt the eyes of the man in the portrait were looking at her. Colonel Fish's presence was always strongest in the front parlor, where a red velvet eighteenth-century English tubchair sat in front of a bookcase containing old volumes of Shakespeare and an assortment of history books. Mrs. Dudley said that anyone who sat in the chair sensed that this was really Colonel Fish's chair. Rarely did the ghost appear anywhere else in the house, although sometimes people who walked down the stairs at the end of the hall experienced a slight tightness in the muscles, as if someone were walking behind them. Could it be that Colonel Fish is still inspecting the improvements being made in his house?

The Bealls 1860 Restaurant's Ghostly Fare

Sorrow hangs like a pall over the Beall House. The lives of the occupants recall the fall of royal families in ancient Greek tragedies. The house was built in Macon by a wealthy cotton planter, Nathan Beall, in 1860. The familial bliss of Nathan and his wife, Martha, son George, and daughter Juliet was cut short by the Civil War. On March 4, 1862, eighteen-year-old George enlisted in the 47th Regiment of the Georgia Infantry. By February 1863, he had become one of thousands of young soldiers listed as missing. Around the same time that George disappeared, Juliet's husband, Dr. George C. Griffin, was ordered to report for duty as an assistant surgeon in Macon. He vanished as well between Petersburg and Macon. For the rest of her life, Juliet sat in the study on the second floor, where she stared out the window in the hope that some day her husband would return home.

Adding to Nathan Beall's sorrow was the destruction of his cotton fields by General Sherman's army. Penniless after the war, Beall was forced to sell his home in 1865 for the then princely sum of $30,000 to Georgia's richest man, Leonidas A. Jordan. Jordan and his wife, Julia, were perfectly happy living in the home for twenty-six years. But then on December 3, 1891, the former Beall home again became a house of sorrows when Julia died of influenza and pneumonia. Devastated by the loss of the most important person in his life, the sixty-eight-year-old widower believed he was truly blessed when a friend introduced him to twenty-one-year-old Ilah Dunlap, who looked almost exactly as Julia had at that age. After making Ilah the sole beneficiary of his vast fortune, Leonidas married Ilah two weeks later.

For the next six years, Leonidas became a virtual prisoner in his own home. Ilah refused to allow any of his friends and relatives to visit him, even after his health began to decline. He died alone in the house in 1899. Ilah's true feelings for her late husband were revealed when she buried him with only a modest county marker. She also sold off all of Leonidas and Julia's engraved silverware. Ilah, on the other hand, was buried in the largest mausoleum in Macon's Rose Hill Cemetery in 1939. In 1993, the historic home was converted into the Bealls 1860 Restaurant. Enough unexplainable activity has occurred in the restaurant to convince management and staff that restless spirits must be afoot.

The most visible evidence of an otherworldly presence is a large, brown stain in the concrete directly beneath the study window. Many years ago, a woman jumped to her death from a second-story window. Efforts to remove the two-foot stain with bleach and other solvents have proven unsuccessful over the years. Even if the staff is able to remove the stain, it always reappears.

Many staff members have experienced what seems to be poltergeist activity. Barbara Duffey reports in *Banshees, Bugles and Belles* that one night, a waiter was fixing drinks when the ice cubes seemed to hop out of the glasses onto the bar. Every time he placed the cubes back in the glasses, they jumped out again. On another occasion, a bartender noticed a young girl in a white dress sitting on one of the stools. After a few minutes, she vanished. Employees of the restaurant have also seen glasses fly off the counter and books fall off the shelves into a pile. Chandeliers have been known to flicker on and off. The most dramatic incident occurred in 1993, not long after the restaurant opened. The waiters were going about their business when all at once, all of the pipes began to shake. The noise became so loud that some waiters placed their hands over their ears. After the shaking stopped, the employees believed that they had experienced an earthquake. When they realized that the tremors had taken place very close to the anniversary of Julia's death, however, some of them offered a paranormal explanation. Or could the poltergeist activity be a manifestation of Leonidas's anger at the way he was mistreated by Ilah, on whom he had lavished so much wealth and affection?

The Mischievous Ghost at the Windsor Hotel

The small town of Americus is probably the last place you would expect to find a luxury hotel like the Windsor. It was built by a group of investors with the idea that it would attract hunters and "snowbirds" eager to escape the winter blasts of the North. The grand opening of the hotel, named after local businessman John. T.

Windsor, was heralded with a great ball on June 16, 1892. In 1899, Charles A. Fricker bought the Windsor at auction and completely refurbished the interior. Fricker's improvements failed to revive the hotel's popularity, however, so it was converted into an apartment building. When the Windsor closed its doors in 1974, its last owner, Howard Dayton, donated the old hotel to the city of Americus. After $5.8 million was spent restoring the Windsor in 1990, it finally reopened in 1991 with a grand celebration. In its heyday, the Windsor attracted a host of celebrities, including William Jennings Bryan, Theodore Roosevelt, John L. Sullivan, Al Capone, Jessica Tandy, and President Jimmy Carter.

Paranormal activity has been reported in the Windsor Hotel, most of it taking place on the third floor. Some guests claim to have seen the silhouette of a woman in a long, black gown in the mirror. Many people believe that some of the men and women who worked there are still on the job. One of the overly dedicated spirits appears to be that of Floyd Lowery, a very friendly elevator operator who worked at the Windsor for forty years. A more playful ghost is a little girl who has been heard and seen laughing and running down the hall. Her mother, who was the Windsor's head housekeeper in the early 1890s, lived there with her daughter. One night, the woman was thrown down an elevator shaft to her death. Some staff members believe that the ghosts of the unfortunate woman and her daughter are very protective of the hotel's guests. In *Georgia Ghostly Getaways*, Kathleen Walls writes that one evening, a hospital employee named Ida Robinson was carrying a tray down a hallway when a little girl walked right past her. Sensing that something was wrong, Ida turned around just in time to witness the child vanishing into the walls. Not long afterward, Ida had just removed a salad bowl from a kitchen cabinet when the telephone rang in another room. When Ida returned to the kitchen, she was surprised to find that someone had filled the salad bowl to the brim.

Even though locals and staff have claimed for years that the Windsor Hotel is haunted, it received verification on Sunday, August 13, when a group of Tallahassee paranormal investigators called the Big Bend Ghost Trackers spent the night at the hotel. At 9 P.M., one of the group's EVP experts recorded what seemed to be a spectral voice in the kitchen. Then at 10 P.M., Betty Davis, the director of the group, began her investigation of the third floor. She began whistling "A Tisket, A Tasket" in the hallway to attract the attention of the ghost of the little girl and was shocked to discover that her thermometer picked up a drop in temperature of 4 degrees. At the same time, one of the video cameras captured three orbs moving down the hallway in a skipping fashion. Another camera photographed a snakelike streak of mist moving down the hallway. Not long thereafter, Davis and some of the other members of the group witnessed a lightbulb that had been unscrewed for filming purposes turn on by itself. A few members of the group also heard the sounds of a baby crying and a woman talking. When the activity died down at 3 A.M., the investigators dismantled their equipment. After returning to their base and analyzing the evidence they collected, they determined that the Windsor Hotel was indeed haunted.

Memory Hill Cemetery's Restless Dead

When plans were being drawn for the city of Millidgeville in December 1804, four squares of twenty acres each were set aside. The South Square was designated for public use. The Methodist church was built in the South Square in 1809, along with the church cemetery. After the Methodist church moved to Statehouse Square, the entire South Square became the Millidgeville City Cemetery. "Memory Hill" was officially attached to the cemetery's original name in 1945. Many famous people are buried here, including author Flannery O'Connor, statesman Carl Vinson, outlaw Bill Miner, and noted scientist Charles Holmes Herty. A number of slave graves and the graves of patients who resided in Millidgeville's "lunatic asylum" can also be found here. You might expect a cemetery with such a diverse population of people to contain a really interesting number of ghosts. According to local residents, it does.

One of the most mischievous ghosts in Memory Hill Cemetery, if the legends can be believed, is that of Mrs. Dixie Haygood. Born in Millidgeville in 1862, Dixie was said to have displayed supernatural powers when she was in the throes of epileptic seizures. Known as "the Little Georgia Magnet," Dixie performed on stages in the United States and Europe under the stage name Annie Abbott. She even appeared before the royal heads of Europe, including the prince of Wales, the tsar of Russia, and Queen Victoria.

It was said that Dixie could lift men into midair simply by placing her hands on their heads. During one show, three men held on to a pool cue. They were unable to force it to the ground while she was touching it. Four strong men were unable to move her while she stood on one foot. She even lifted four men sitting on a chair by placing her hands on the chair. By the time Dixie Haywood died on November 23, 1915, she was a patient at Central State Hospital for the Mentally Insane. According to some of the staff at the hospital, Dixie cursed the town and everything in it just before she died. Some local residents believe that proof of the curse can be found in Memory Hill Cemetery. In *Banshees, Bugles and Belles,* Barbara Duffey reports that every year just before Christmas, a sinkhole appears in the Yates family plot, located next to Dixie's grave. The hole is so deep that the tombstones of Mr. Yates and his daughter have been completely swallowed up. The city has tried to fill up the depression with cement and gravel, but the hole always shows up again the next Christmas, on cue.

Stories have also grown up around a wrought-iron fence surrounding one particular grave. It is said that the man who is buried there had the faces of imps fashioned into the fence for protection from evil spirits after he died. Some people swear that on All Hallow's Eve, the imps howl and moan.

Probably the strangest legend concerns the crypt of Mr. J. A. Fish. After his wife and daughter died of typhus in 1872, he became so despondent that he carried a rocking chair inside the tomb and bricked himself in. Visitors who knock on the door sometimes hear a faint knocking sound coming from the inside. It is also said that for many years, children would knock on the tomb and ask, "What are you doing, Mr. Fish?" The reply was always the same: "Nothing at all."

The Lovely Ghost of Panola Hall

With its huge Doric columns, nine-foot windows, and heavy parapet concealing the almost completely flat roof, Panola Hall stands out from most of the other homes in Eatonton, and the rest of Georgia, for that matter. James M. Broadfield built this Greek Revival house for Henry Trippe in 1854. Trippe, a planter from Putnam County, wanted his wife, Elizabeth, and two daughters to live in the finest house available in Eatonton. The discovery of a sword, shotgun, and musket inside an attic wall in 1979 supports the legend that Confederate soldiers hid in the mansion during the Civil War.

In 1891, Dr. Benjamin Hunt bought the house after marrying Louisa Prudden of Eatonton. The Hunts named their new home Panola Hall and made a few changes of their own. Dr. Hunt, who was an amateur horticulturist as well as a businessman and scientist, planted a number of rare plants around his home, many of which are still growing. In 1922, the University of Georgia recognized Hunt's experiments in dairy farming and botany with an honorary doctor of science degree. Louisa was a very cultured woman who wrote poetry in her free time. She could not have imagined when she and her husband moved into Panola Hall that they would be sharing their beautiful home with a beautiful ghost.

Louisa first saw the ghost soon after she and her husband moved in. She was sitting in her parlor reading when the shimmering figure of a young woman in a white dress materialized. Louisa tried to speak to the apparition, but she disappeared. According to Barbara Duffey in *Banshees, Bugles and Belles*, Louisa kept the knowledge of the ghost's existence to herself until an Ohio millionaire named Nelson saw the apparition on his way upstairs. When he asked why the girl did not show up for dinner, Louisa told him that she was dead. Thinking that his hosts were fooling him, he wrote several love letters to the phantom, whom Louisa called Sylvia. Louisa left the letters in the bedroom where she first saw Sylvia. She became so attached to the lovely spirit living in her home that she wrote a poem entitled "An Ode to Sylvia," in which she described Sylvia as having "smile on lip and rose in hair."

Sylvia has been seen by other people as well. In *Ghost Stories of Georgia*, Chris Wangler reports that in the 1920s, a librarian named Alice Wardwell was sitting on the front step of the library across the street from Panola Hall one summer evening. As she glanced at the open windows of the Hunts' living room, she noticed that Louisa was sewing and Benjamin was reading. The couple was oblivious to the fact that a beautiful, dark-haired young woman in a white dress was standing directly over Dr. Hunt's shoulder. Alice asked a group of young girls who were walking into the library to tell her what they saw in the living room. They too saw a young woman in a white dress standing behind Dr. Hunt. The next day, Alice asked him who his charming visitor was. He replied that it must have been their ghost, because they had had no visitors that day.

Sylvia also appeared on the day Louisa Hunt died. In 1941, a longtime friend of Louisa's, Bessie Butler, told an interviewer for the *Atlanta Journal* magazine that as Louisa lay dying in 1929, she was walking into an upstairs bedroom when she heard very soft footsteps behind her and a voice saying, "Miss Bessie. Oh, Miss Bessie." The unexpected appearance of the family ghost frightened Bessie so much that she ran downstairs and told Dr. Hunt what had happened. He replied that if Bessie had stayed upstairs, she might have received a message from Sylvia.

Ghostly activity in Panola Hall continued even after the old mansion was passed down to different owners. Mr. and Mrs. M. L. Liles, who purchased the house in 1946 and lived there until 1981, said that the lights turned off and on by themselves. On occasion, they heard a dripping sound, but they never located its source. One of the Liles's boarders complained that sometimes at night, something pulled the covers off him while he was sleeping. As Mr. Liles lay dying, several people claimed to have seen Sylvia, including a neighbor who swore that Sylvia crossed her lawn and walked into her house. Even author Barbara Duffey says she made Sylvia's acquaintance in April 1995, when she visited the house to take some pictures. After she finished photographing the interior of the house, she stood on the stairs and called Sylvia's name several times. She was astonished when she heard a faint whistle. Duffey described the sound as "a child's feeble attempts at practicing his first sounds through pursed lip." The caretaker told Duffey that he never heard anything unusual in the old home. While standing in Sylvia's room, Duffey photographed what appears to be a thin wisp of mist rising from a shutter, perhaps evidence of whatever's haunting Panola Hall.

The Werewolf of Talbot County

In the 1840s, a wealthy widow named Mildred Owen lived in a backwoods region of Talbot County, a heavily wooded area of northwest Georgia, with her four children. One daughter, Isabella, was an introverted child with dark, shaggy hair and very pointed teeth. She loved to read, especially the books on the supernatural that her mother had brought back from Europe. Following a trip to Europe with her family, Isabella was plagued with bouts of insomnia. On nights when she could not sleep, the girl began roaming the countryside. Before long, farmers began finding sheep with their throats ripped out. It is said that Isabella listened intently when neighbors warned her mother that her sheep were in danger as well.

One night, Isabella's sister Sarah awoke to see her walking out the front door, followed by her mother. Intrigued, Sarah grabbed a gun and followed them through the woods and across the field at a safe distance. Unknown to Sarah and the other two women, a posse was combing the fields in search of the beast. When Sarah reached the sheep pasture, she was appalled at the scene before her in the moonlight. Her sister Isabella was about to pounce on a sheep with a knife in her hand. When Mildred ordered Isabella to stop at once, she turned her wrathful gaze upon her mother and growled. Sarah raised her gun but was unable to fire at her sister. Suddenly, the air erupted with the sound of gunfire. Isabella swooned and collapsed in a heap upon the ground.

The next morning, lying in bed, Sarah learned that Isabella had been shot in the hand by a member of the posse, just as she was about to attack her mother. After her wound was treated, Isabella was sent to Europe, supposedly to visit relatives. Actually, Isabella was placed in the care of a physician who specialized in the treatment of lycanthropy—assuming the form or characteristics of a wolf. She returned home a few months later. Locals assumed that she was cured because no more sheep were mutilated and killed during the night. Isabella, who never married, died in 1911 at age seventy and was buried in the Owen and Holmes Cemetery in Woodland.

Gravity Hill's Helpful Ghost

One of the most mysterious locations in Georgia is Gravity Hill near Bonaire. To find Gravity Hill, take State Route 96 across the Ocmulgee River. When you come to the intersection of U.S. Route 129, turn left and drive over the first hill. Stop the car at the bottom of the next hill and put it in neutral. Magically, your car will coast *up* the hill.

Unlike Magic Hill on Route 41 near Manchester, where the same weirdness occurs, Gravity Hill's phenomenon has a story behind it. Legend has it that in the early 1800s, a witch charged travelers a toll to use the section of road leading up to what is now called Gravity Hill. Once the witch was paid, she helped her customers mount the steep hill. Not only did local residents grow accustomed to having a witch living in their midst, but they even called upon her for help when the area was beset by a severe drought.

After the witch died in 1850, locals wanted to show their gratitude by burying her in a church cemetery, but the minister refused to lay her to rest in sacred ground. Undeterred, they buried the witch in the swamp and marked her grave with an impressive five-foot-high monument made of a pile of rocks. People say that to show her gratitude, she now gives drivers a push up Gravity Hill, just as she did nearly two hundred years ago after receiving her toll.

Coastal Georgia

GEORGIA'S ATLANTIC COASTLINE EXTENDS MORE THAN 100 MILES. IF one were to include the river mouths, bays, and offshore islands, the coastline would measure 2,344 miles. Except for St. Catherine's Island, all of Coastal Georgia's golden isles have been developed in the twentieth and twenty-first centuries. But long before Jekyll Island and others became playgrounds for the rich, Georgia's islands were inhabited by tribes of Native Americans. Then in the seventeenth and eighteenth centuries, Spanish and English settlers claimed the islands as their own. Not surprisingly, the culture clashes created by the arrival of so many different types of people have produced a wealth of ghost stories.

The Ghostly Choir of St. Catherine's Island

Music is part of our lives. We hear it on car radios, in department stores and restaurants, on iPods, on the computer—almost every place we go has background music playing somewhere. But long before the invention of the phonograph and radio, people living on St. Catherine's Island were being entertained by music from beyond the grave.

Two centuries before James Oglethorpe founded Savannah in 1733, a Spanish explorer named Lucas Vasquez de Allyon founded the first mission on St. Catherine's Island in 1526. His mission failed within a year, and Pedro Mendez de Aviles, the Spanish governor of St. Augustine, tried again in 1565. The Santa Catalina Mission on St. Catherine's Island was the first of thirty-eight missions established across the southeast. The Franciscan friars baptized, doctored, and disciplined the Guale Indians on the island. They also taught them church ritual and antiphonal chants in Latin. In his letters, the head friar had high praise for the young Guale males in the choir, whose high voices blended well with those of the older missionaries. The small missionary outpost was burned in 1597, during a revolt by the Guale Indians, but the Spanish rebuilt it eight years later. Under pressure by the British, the Spanish finally abandoned the Santa Catalina Mission in 1680.

According to Alabama folklorist Kathryn Tucker Windham, the influence of the missionaries on the Guale Indians can still be heard. In *13 Georgia Ghosts and Jeffrey,* Windham writes of an eerie experience Mrs. Courtney Thorpe had in her home on St. Catherine's Island in the early 1930s. She was relaxing on her porch one evening when she heard a chorus of male voices. The voices were audible for a good five minutes, then faded away. The singing reminded her of the chanting she had heard at the Cathedral of St. John the Baptist in Savannah, where she occasionally went with friends. When Mrs. Thorpe heard the singing again a few days later, she recalled the early efforts of the Spanish missionaries to Christianize the Guale Indians. After researching the history of the Spanish presence on the island in the sixteenth and seventeenth centuries, she became convinced that the chanting she had heard was the spectral singing of the ghostly choir of the Santa Catalina Mission.

Because the choir never "performed" when her friends were sitting on the porch, Mrs. Thorpe decided to record the phantom voices, using blank records and a recorder. One night, the singing became so distinct that Mrs. Thorpe could make out every single Latin word. She turned on the recorder and basked in the beauty of the singing. Suddenly, Mrs. Thorpe smelled smoke; her recorder was on fire! She threw a small rug over the recorder and extinguished the fire, but her recording was destroyed. Mrs. Thorpe never heard the singing of the Franciscan monks and their Indian converts again.

The Playful Ghost of Orange Hall

Visitors centers in cities and small towns are often located in historic houses. Such is the case of Orange Hall on St. Marys Island. Visitors expecting to find a bright orange building will be disappointed. Orange Hall was named for the sour orange grove behind the house. The history of the old mansion is sketchy. Construction on Orange Hall began in the late 1820s and probably continued into the early 1830s. One story has it that John Wood built the house for his daughter Jane Wood Pratt. According to another version of the story, Wood sold the property to his son-in-law Horace Pratt, and Pratt built Orange Hall for his second wife, Isabel Drysdale Pratt. Research conducted by the Department of the Interior has revealed, however, that the core of the house was constructed in the 1830s, and the size of the home was expanded between 1846 and 1857. In 1846, James Mongin Smith acquired the home, and he sold it in 1856 to the mayor of St. Marys, Francis M. Adams. Orange Hall was spared destruction during the Civil War when it became the headquarters of a squad of Union troops. After the Civil War, it passed through a series of owners. Then in 1933, St. Marys Kraft converted the mansion into an apartment building for its workers. The plant deeded Orange Hall to the city of St. Marys in 1960. Regardless of who owned Orange Hall, it has always been a center of social activity. Many people on the island believe it is the center of paranormal activity as well.

Don Farrant, author of *Ghosts of the Georgia Coast*, believes that three ghosts are haunting Orange Hall. A paranormal researcher who visited the old mansion told the staff that he saw the apparition of a young man in a military uniform standing in front of the fireplace. Only the upper torso of the ghost was visible. As the ghost hunter walked toward the specter, the ghost became increasingly transparent. On another occasion, a woman who had received special permission to videotape inside the house got more than she had bargained for. When she reviewed the tape, she realized that she had captured the image of an elderly man dressed in nineteenth-century clothing standing in a doorway.

The third ghost has been identified as the spirit of Jane Pratt, Horace's daughter, who died of yellow fever when she was six years old. According to Farrant, Baby Jane, as she has come to be called, has been sighted playing with a doll in her bedroom. She also has been credited with moving her doll from one place to another and rumpling her bed. Author Nancy Roberts says that tourists have seen a little girl wearing a white dress and blue ribbons skipping along the walk, passing them on the stairs, and sitting in a chair and looking out her window toward Wheeler Street. Chances are that if you stop by St. Marys visitors center, you too will be welcomed by the cheerful little spirit of Orange Hall.

St. Simons Island's Wandering Ghost

Stories of lost love are among the saddest and most enduring legends in any culture. Such a tale is the tragic story of Mary MacRae. Mary and her parents, Angus and Martha MacRae, made the long voyage from Glasgow, Scotland, to Savannah in the early 1800s. By the time she reached the New World, however, Mary's parents and brother had died from the smallpox that ravaged the ship. Left utterly alone in a strange country, thirteen-year-old Mary was overcome with sorrow and fear as she huddled inside a crowded church. Fortunately, a newlywed couple named Amelia and Jeremy Grant, who also had just arrived from Glasgow, took pity on the poor girl and invited her to accompany them to the Marston Plantation near Savannah where they had found work. Mary so enjoyed living with the Grants and caring for the horses in the stable that she almost forgot that she was an orphan.

Mary's life changed drastically when a wealthy cotton planter from St. Simons Island named Raymond Demere visited the plantation. He lured her to the island by telling her that a young woman like her could do well at Groves Plantation. When Mary arrived at the island, she was saddened at the thought of leaving the Grants, but the natural beauty of the plantation made the adjustment much easier. Mary also found herself attracted to Mr. Demere's younger son, the tall, athletic Raymond Jr. Unlike his more serious-minded brother Joseph, Raymond enjoyed riding, sailing, and attending parties. By the time Mary was eighteen, she was head over heels in love with the dashing young man.

Unfortunately, Raymond's father felt the same way about Mary, who had developed into a beautiful young woman with flaming red hair. Realizing that Mary missed the stable where she had worked with the Grants, Mr. Demere offered to give her his best mare. Mary was flattered but turned down the gift, stating that she did not even know how to ride very well. The next day, Mary found herself receiving her first riding lesson from her employer. While they were eating a picnic lunch under an oak tree, Raymond Jr. rode up on his horse, swept Mary up on his saddle, and rode off. After returning to the stable, the young man professed his love for Mary and told her he wanted to leave Groves Plantation with her. Mary and Raymond Jr. returned to the house just as Mr. Demere was walking his horse back to the stall. Mr. and Mrs. Demere listened patiently to their son's declaration of his love for Mary and his intention to marry her. When he had finished, Mr. Demere informed him that he would cut him out of his will if he lowered himself by marrying a servant girl. Controlling his anger, Raymond Jr. turned to Mary and told her that he was going to some other town, such as Brunswick or Darien, and would return for her later. He then charged out of house, slamming doors behind him.

Mary was alarmed, not just because her lover stood to lose his inheritance, but also because a hurricane was on the way. She rushed to her room and lit a lantern with embers from the fireplace; then she donned her cloak and marched out into the storm. Rain slashed her face as she made her way to the dock. Finding only the rope that Raymond Jr. had used to tie up his boat, she frantically called his name, although nothing could be heard above the howling wind. Holding out her lantern before her, Mary made her way along the edge of the inlet. Suddenly she stopped walking and stared down at her feet. Mary screamed as she realized she was looking at pieces of Raymond's little boat floating in the water.

No one knows what happened to Mary after that moment of recognition. Some people believe that she walked over to a nearby cliff and jumped off the edge. Others believe that she walked into the surf and drowned herself. For several days, the Demere family searched for Mary and Raymond Jr., but to no avail. Their bodies were never found.

For generations, residents of St. Simons Island have seen a spectral figure they have identified as the spirit of Mary MacRae. Don Farrant says in *Ghosts of the Georgia Coast* that in 1940, the ghost that has come be known as Mary the Wanderer appeared to John Symons and his wife, who were visiting the island. At 2 A.M., they

decided to cool off by driving along the beach. They were headed toward the airport when they beheld what appeared to be a woman wearing a long, white dress and veil standing beside a horse. The windows of the car were beginning to fog, so John lowered his window for a better look. He could still see the woman and the horse standing by the road, but in a few moments they were gone.

A wraith that could be another incarnation of Mary the Wanderer was seen a few years later. A former third-grade teacher named Carolyn Butler was living in a house not far from the route Mary had taken in search of her boyfriend. One day Carolyn was standing in front of her house when something that looked like a white blob appeared a few feet away. Her dog, Boots, was so frightened by the apparition that he hid inside a nearby store. She tried to coax the little dog to return home, but he always ran off again after a few hours.

The most dramatic sighting of Mary the Wanderer occurred one night in the mid-1950s. An Eastern Airlines Martin 303 was approaching Malcolm McKinnon Airport when the copilot exclaimed over the radio that a woman wearing a long, white dress was sitting on a horse on the airfield. The radio operator from the flight service station replied that he did not see anything unusual on the airfield. The copilot and the radio operator continued arguing back and forth, until finally the copilot was instructed not to land and to fly to Jacksonville instead.

Mary the Wanderer's tragic life has made such an impact on St. Simons Island that she is the only ghost in the South who has had a road named after her. Cutting through the oaks southeast of Demere Road near Charter Hospital is a narrow dirt road called Mary Wan Road. The road does not appear on a map, and the road sign was stolen years ago, but local residents are still convinced that the 560-foot-long stretch of road traces part of the path taken by Mary the Wanderer during her ill-fated search for her lost love.

The Ghost in Room 8

At first sight, the Riverview Hotel on the banks of the St. Marys River looks more like a relic of the Old West than an island resort hotel. Built in 1916 across from the Cumberland Island Ferry office, the Riverview Hotel is known for its double veranda and the deer heads mounted on the walls. It was constructed with a protective coating of tabby, a cement made from a mixture of oyster shells, sand, lime, and water. In the 1920s, the hotel was purchased by Sally Brandon and her two sisters, Semora and Ethel. To this day, the Riverview Hotel is still owned and operated by the Brandon family.

According to Jerry Brandon, the present owner, one guest has refused to check out for decades. Nancy Roberts in *Georgia Ghosts* reports that Jerry was a child when he and his family lived in the hotel in the 1950s. At the time, the hotel was closed to the public. One day, Jerry's sister and her friend Jeanie Porter decided to play on the second floor of the hotel, which had been shut off for years. As they ran down the deserted hallway, the girls tried to frighten each other by screaming as loudly as they could. Each time they passed a room, they opened the door and made moaning noises. Tiring of this game, they ventured into the north wing, which neither Sally nor Jeanie had explored before. The girls were reading off the room numbers when all at once a figure wearing a broad-brimmed hat and long, black coat appeared in front of Room 8. His face was a ghastly white, and his eyes were jet black. The frightened girls ran out of the wing and down the stairs as fast as they could.

Not long before, in the mid-1950s, a number of sightings had occurred in Room 8. A man was sleeping in the room when he felt someone pulling his leg. He was so terrified that he hastily packed his suitcase and checked into another hotel. Jerry's parents were not surprised; another guest had had a similar experience in the same room. A few years later, during a power outage, only the light in front of Room 8 remained lit. This also happened to be the same spot where Sally and Jeanie had seen the apparition. The identity of the ghost remains a mystery. Like previous generations of Brandons, Jerry has learned to live with him, and he expects his guests to do the same.

An Extended Visit at the Jekyll Island Club Hotel

Jekyll Island was attracting visitors long before it became an upscale resort. As early as 2500 B.C., small groups of hunter-gatherers paddled over to the barrier island off Georgia's southern coast to take advantage of the abundant plants and wildlife. The Guale Indians arrived in 1540 A.D. and remained there for several hundred years. Although evidence shows that the Spanish did make contact with the Guale Indians, the British established the first permanent settlement on Jekyll Island in 1734. James Oglethorpe renamed the island in honor of his friend Sir Joseph Jekyll. Over the next forty years, a number of different people owned Jekyll Island, including a small group of French investors called the Sapelo Company. The next visitors to Jekyll Island were slaves who were brought to the island to pick cotton.

Jekyll Island did not really become a tourist attraction until Newton Finney and his brother-in-law John Eugene DuBignon devised a plan to build an exclusive social club there in 1879. DuBignon eventually purchased the club and sold it to the newly incorporated Jekyll Island Club, whose fifty-three original investors included Marshall Field, J. P. Morgan, William K. Vanderbilt, and Henry Hyde. Construction began in 1886, and the club officially opened in January 1888. The island soon became the private playground of America's wealthiest families, including the Pulitzers, Vanderbilts, and Rockefellers. Between 1888 and 1928, the club's wealthy members built winter homes, or cottages, as they came to be known. The Jekyll Island Club flourished into the 1930s, but membership plummeted during the Great Depression. The U.S. government completely evacuated the island in World War II because of the threat of enemy submarines just off the coast. The state of Georgia purchased the island in 1947 and converted it into a state park, but an investment firm leased several club properties on the island and transformed them into the Jekyll Island Club Hotel, one of the finest luxury hotels in the country. According to reports from the staff, some guests are taking a very extended visit.

Legend has it that one of Jekyll Island's very first guests was not even alive at the time. The club's first president, General Lloyd

Aspinwall, died on September 4, 1886, more than a year before the club officially opened. The day after Aspinwall's death, a few guests swore that they saw him walking along the Riverfront Veranda.

Another ghost at the hotel is Samuel Spencer, president of the Southern Railroad Company, who was a frequent guest at the hotel in the early 1900s. Spencer always stayed in the same room, an apartment with mahogany furniture, a wide veranda, and a marble fireplace. His daily routine consisted of sipping his morning coffee and reading the *Wall Street Journal,* which was always folded in a special way. In 1906, he was killed in a collision between two trains. Ironically, Spencer owned both of the locomotives. Today guests staying in Spencer's room have found their newspaper folded in a strange way or open to the business section. Other guests claim that someone poured coffee into a cup when they were in another room and even drank some of it.

Not all of the ghosts at the Jekyll Island Club Hotel are the spirits of former guests, however. Sheila Turnage, author of *Haunted Inns of the Southeast,* interviewed a former bellman she called Fred, who had a ghostly encounter. He was walking down the second-floor hallway when he saw out of the corner of his eye a bellman wearing the attire of a much earlier time—a pillbox hat and striped pants. The apparition abruptly vanished when Fred tried to look at him head-on. The spectral bellman has been credited with returning dry cleaning to the rooms of groomsmen in several weddings that have been held there. Most people would say that this is the kind of help they definitely do not need.

Ghosts of Ebo Landing: The Long Walk Home

The tragic events that occurred at Ebo Landing on St. Simons Island deserve to be much better known than they are. In late 1802, a group of Igbo tribesmen from southern Nigeria were captured by native slavers. They were taken to a waiting ship, the *York,* which transported them to Skidaway Island just outside Savannah. Two Georgia planters, Thomas Spaulding and John Couper, paid $500 each for seventy-five slaves. In mid-May 1803, the slaves were placed on a ship named the *Morovia,* which brought them to Dunbar Creek on

St. Simons Island. Before the ship landed, the slaves revolted, and two crewmembers and Couper's overseer were so panic-stricken that they jumped overboard and drowned. Suddenly, the captain's own slave shocked everyone on board by walking into Dunbar Creek. Then the Igbo chief began singing, "The water brought us here, and the water will take us away," in his native language. All of the other slaves followed suit and marched into the creek. At least ten died, preferring death over the living hell of slavery.

Many people living on St. Simons Island believe that Ebo Landing is haunted by the spirits of the drowned slaves, whose chant, "The water brought us here, and the water will take us away," can still be heard occasionally on fog-shrouded nights. In *Ghosts of the Georgia Coast*, Don Farrant writes of a woman who had a close encounter with the ghosts of the slaves. He says that one windy, moonlit night, a woman was driving her car along Frederica Road on St. Simons Island. All at once, she caught a glimpse of four or six men at the side of the road. The men were dressed in rags and barefoot. They were all shackled together, the right wrist and ankle of one to the left wrist and ankle of another. In a matter of seconds, the entire group of men disappeared.

Farrant also reports the experience a woman living in a large residential area close to Dunbar Creek had in her house. She was sleeping in her bedroom when she woke up and saw an indistinct human form. The man's face bore a "fierce and grim" appearance. He vanished after a moment or two. One can only hope that the restless dead of Ebo Landing will find peace some day.

The Tipsy Ghost of Dungeness Mansion

Although people have lived on Cumberland Island for thousands of years, it remains one of Georgia's best kept secrets. Archaeological evidence shows that Native Americans were living on the island four thousand years ago. At least seven native villages were still thriving on Cumberland Island in 1566 when Spanish explorers arrived. Between 1566 and 1670, the Spanish built several missions and forts on the island that they called San Pedro, but no evidence of any Spanish settlements remain.

When British General James Oglethorpe arrived in Georgia in the 1730s, he renamed the island Cumberland Island in honor of the duke of Cumberland. The British formed a settlement called Berrimacke on Cumberland Island, as well as a series of forts. By 1775, the British had completely abandoned the island. Then in 1796, Catherine Greene, the wife of Revolutionary War hero General Nathanael Greene, built the first Dungeness Mansion on an Indian shell mound. The magnificent four-story tabby mansion became the center of high society in Georgia during the first half of the nineteenth century. In 1866, Dungeness fell into disrepair and was burned to the ground, possibly by freed slaves.

Fourteen years later, steel magnate Andrew Carnegie purchased most of Cumberland Island. In 1884, Thomas Carnegie and his wife, Lucy, built a new mansion on the foundations of the first Dungeness. Carnegie's Dungeness had forty outbuildings, a pool house, golf course, and squash court. Five generations of the Carnegie family continued using Dungeness as a retreat until it burned down in 1959, leaving only a charred ruin. In 1972, the Carnegie family sold Dungeness and most of its holdings on Cumberland Island to the National Park Service. Although only a few vestiges of fine living remain on the island, it seems that one of the Dungeness socialites still makes an occasional appearance.

At one time, a polo field was adjacent to the mansion. Don Farrant writes in *Ghosts of the Georgia Coast* that one night in the early 1900s, a group of polo players was attending one of the Carnegies' evening parties. Later that night, one of the players discovered that the bar had run out of his favorite wine. Enraged, the drunken guest staggered out of the mansion, mounted his horse, and galloped off to the servants' quarters down the road, where he believed the wine could be found. Because of the night gloom and his inebriated state, the polo player did not see a low overhanging limb of one of the massive oak trees that lined the road. The limb struck the polo player in the head, knocking him off his horse onto the road. He was killed instantly. Some residents of Cumberland Island believe that the man lay dead for several days along the roadside before visitors discovered his corpse. In the early 1990s, a naturalist was in one of the servants' quarters when she saw a very fit-looking young man walk down the stairs from the second floor. He was wearing a white shirt and dark pants, the customary attire of polo players at the turn of the century. Neither of her associates saw the apparition. After a moment's reflection, she recalled the legend of the drunken polo player, who apparently is still looking for his liquor in the servants' quarters.

Another strange occurrence is reported by Barbara Duffey in *Angels and Apparitions*. A maintenance foreman for the Sanitation Department named Joe Peacock told Duffey that in the early 1980s, on cool nights when the moon was full, five or six owls sat on top of the ruined chimneys and hooted. He noticed that these meetings occurred at least once a month. By 1996, the owls had ceased congregating at Dungeness Mansion. Peacock wondered if the birds had been possessed by the spirits of the Carnegie family or their guests.

St. Simons Lighthouse

Today most of America's lighthouses are nothing more than picturesque relics of the past. In 1807, however, when James Gould of Massachusetts built the first lighthouse on St. Simons Island, lighthouses were the only way ships at sea could navigate along America's treacherous Atlantic coastline. Gould built the seventy-five-foot tower, constructed of tabby, on a four-acre piece of land owned by a planter named John Couper. Gould was appointed lighthouse keeper in 1810, and he held this position until he retired in 1837.

During the Civil War, the Confederate Army destroyed the lighthouse to keep it out of the hands of the Union Army. Construction of a second, bigger lighthouse—104 feet high with 129 steps— began in 1867 just west of the original structure. The second lighthouse was not completed until September 1862 because an outbreak of malaria took the lives of the designer, noted architect Charles Cluskey, and most of his crew. When fuel for the lamps was switched from lard to kerosene, a brick oil house was added in 1890. The lighthouse began using electricity in 1934. The U.S. Coast Guard now owns the lighthouse, although it has been leased to the Georgia Historical Society. Generations of lighthouse keepers have believed that a violent incident that occurred in 1880 has left an indelible impression on the old lighthouse.

In 1880, John Stevens was hired as assistant to the old lighthouse keeper, a contentious old man named Fred Osborne. Osborne was a perfectionist who schooled the young man in the finer details of lighthouse keeping. As time passed, the relationship between the two men became strained. Then on Sunday morning, February 29, 1880, Osborne's patronizing became intolerable. As the older man commenced to relieve his assistant, he complained that Stevens had done a poor job of polishing the prisms of the light. A heated exchange of words soon followed. Finally, Osborne told Stevens, "Let's settle this outside." Osborne climbed down the steps first. By the time Stevens had reached the last step, Osborne was standing a hundred feet away from the doorway. As Stevens walked toward Osborne, the lighthouse keeper drew a pistol. Sensing the need to defend himself, Stevens rushed back inside the lighthouse and came out holding a double-barreled shotgun, which was loaded with buckshot. Stevens raised his shotgun and fired; only four pellets struck Osborne, but one penetrated his abdomen. Stevens rushed Osborne to the hospital in Brunswick, telling the doctors that the shooting was accidental. Stevens worked double shifts until Osborne died a week later. The sheriff took Stevens into custody, but he was permitted to keep his job because an immediate replacement could not be found. Stevens was eventually acquitted because no witnesses to the shooting could be found.

Following Osborne's death, strange sounds were heard in the lighthouse. John Stevens, who continued working in the lighthouse until the following May, said that during storms, he often heard the sound of heavy footsteps on the stairway. Oddly enough, the footsteps never went above the highest landing or below the lowest one. Other lighthouse keepers, such as Carl Svendsen and his wife, also heard the ghostly footsteps. During his twenty-eight years as lighthouse keeper, Svendsen also saw a shadowy form prowling the grounds on several occasions. Svendsen became so spooked that he refused to stand watch alone at night. Even his dog became fearful when the ghostly walking commenced. Some believers in the ghost claim they detect the strong odor of the kerosene that Osborne used in the lamp in the days before electricity. Could it be that Fred Osborne is still standing by in emergency situations when only his expertise can save the day?

Button's Bones

Born in Gloucestershire, England, in 1735, the improbably named Button Gwinnett immigrated to Charleston in the early 1760s, where he was a successful merchant. His desire to become a planter led him to purchase St. Catherine's Island in 1765. But Gwinnett failed to tap the thirty-six-mile tract of land's full agricultural potential and eventually lost St. Catherine's Island. Never one to say die, Gwinnett became a justice of the peace and a member of the Georgia Colonial Assembly. Button achieved national fame after he was elected to the Continental Congress in Philadelphia and eventually became one of the signers of the Declaration of Independence. Gwinnett's promising political career came to an abrupt end a year later when he returned to Savannah and became a speaker of the state assembly. The ramifications of his violent death still resonate in the only real home he ever knew, St. Catherine's Island.

Gwinnett's early demise can be attributed in large part to his military ambitions. He was angered that he was passed over as commander of Georgia's troops in favor of a young general named Lachlan McIntosh, but his hopes were revived somewhat when Archibald Bulloch, first president of the state of Georgia and commander in chief of the army, died suddenly. After the assembly appointed Gwinnett to succeed Bulloch, he took his revenge on McIntosh by having the man's brother arrested as a traitor. Gwinnett also had McIntosh relieved of his command on the grounds that the general, like his brother, betrayed his country. Enraged, McIntosh called Gwinnett a lying scoundrel; Gwinnett retaliated by challenging the general to a duel. The next morning, the two antagonists met on the field of honor near Sea Island Road on the outskirts of Savannah. Both men walked four steps and fired, striking each other in the leg. McIntosh recovered from his wound, but Gwinnett's wound in the thigh became gangrenous. He died three days later at the age of forty-two.

Button Gwinnett's memory had long faded from the national consciousness by 1957, when a retired Savannah school principal named Arthur J. Funk began looking for a painting of Button Gwinnett. Poring through the records at the Chatham County courthouse in Savannah, Funk found that Gwinnett had been buried in the old Colonial Cemetery. With the Park Department's permission, Funk combed the cemetery for traces of Gwinnett grave. Not far from Bulloch's grave, Funk found a piece of stone slab with letters and numbers carved on the surface. He talked the Georgia Historical Commission into sending archaeologist Lewis H. Larson Jr. to investigate the grave. On December 2, Larson uncovered the body of a person five feet, six and a half inches tall with a damaged left femur. While the Historical Commission investigated Funk's claim that these were the remains of Button Gwinnett, Funk placed the bones in a copper-lined oak coffin, which he concealed in a guest room, where it stayed for five years. The Historical Commission had no sooner identified the bones as belonging to Button Gwinnett on September 28, 1959, than the city of Augusta requested that Gwinnett's remains be interred under the Signer's Monument along with two other signers of the Declaration of Independence, Lyman Hall and George Walton. In October 1964, Savannah became Button Gwinnett's official resting place when a new monument was dedicated in Colonial Cemetery to the signer of the Declaration of Independence.

Even though Button Gwinnett's corpse has been buried in Colonial Cemetery for more than two centuries, his spirit has only been seen on St. Catherine's Island. Don Farrant says in *Ghosts of the Georgia Coast* that the phantom hoofbeats of Gwinnett's favorite horse, Chickasaw, can be heard on cloudy nights when thunderstorms are imminent. The apparition of a mounted horseman has been seen riding past the old town of Midway on his way to St. Catherine's Island. Usually the ghostly rider vanishes, then materializes near the wharf where his schooner, *Beggar's Benison,* was once moored. The misty shape of Gwinnett's schooner has also been seen crossing the sound as it transports Gwinnett back to St. Catherine's wharf. Gwinnett's bones may lie in Savannah, but apparently his heart—as well as his ghost—remains on St. Catherine's Island.

Atlanta and Northern Georgia

NORTHERN GEORGIA INCLUDES TWO MAIN LAND REGIONS. COVERING the northwestern corner of Georgia, the Appalachian Plateau ranges from eighteen hundred to two thousand feet above sea level, with heavily wooded areas separated by narrow valleys. Unlike the plateau, the Appalachian Ridge and Valley region has several broad, fertile valleys separated by ridges of sandstone rocks. These valleys are covered by pine and hardwood forests. The fertile soil produces not only vegetables, fruits, and grains, but prime grazing land for cattle as well.

Northern Georgia is a region of paradoxes, owing in large part to its vastness. Atlanta, the largest city in Georgia, is a bustling metropolis, reborn from the ashes of the Civil War. Northwestern Georgia, on the other hand, is blanketed with impenetrable forests and picturesque plantations. The same area that produced the gentle writer Joel Chandler Harris was also the site of the first great Civil War battle in Georgia—Chickamauga. The wide variety of ghost stories from Northern Georgia reflects the vast scope of the region's history and geography. Not surprisingly, more ghost stories can be found in this vast region than anywhere else in that state.

Barnsley Gardens' Mournful Spirits

Strolling through the heirloom gardens that decorate this upscale golf destination, you might find it difficult to believe that a curse hung over Barnsley Gardens. In 1841, cotton factor Godfrey Barnsley ignored an Indian legend warning that the acorn-shaped hill on which he built his house and gardens was an unlucky site. Barnsley's fourteen-room Italian villa called Woodlands was surrounded by magnificent gardens inspired by the designs of Andrew Jackson Downing, America's first great landscape architect. Construction on Woodlands was halted after the death of Barnsley's beloved wife, Julia, in 1845. But Julia's spirit, whom her husband believed communed with him near the fountain in the boxwood garden, persuaded him to resume work on their dream home.

Shortly after Godfrey Barnsley moved into Woodlands, the fortunes of one of the South's wealthiest men continued to plummet. His infant son soon followed his mother in death. Barnsley's second daughter, Adelaide, died in the house in 1858. In 1862, Chinese pirates killed Barnsley's oldest son, Howard, who had ventured to the Orient in search of exotic shrubbery for his father's garden. By the time Woodlands was nearly completed in 1861, the Civil War broke out. In 1864, Confederate Colonel Robert G. Earle was shot down as he rode to Woodlands to warn Barnsley of the Union approach, seemingly yet another victim of the Indian curse. Despite General McPherson's orders forbidding looting at Woodlands, Union soldiers broke windows and china settings, drank all of the vintage wines in the cellar, and smashed an Italian statue.

After the war, the prophecy of ill luck continued to linger over Woodlands. Godfrey Barnsley moved to New Orleans to recoup his fortunes. Before his death in 1873, his daughter Julia and son-in-law Captain James Baltzelle took over Woodlands. James was crushed by a falling tree and killed in 1868. Julia's daughter Adelaide married a chemist named A. A. Saylor and moved into Woodlands, but her husband died soon thereafter, leaving her to raise their two young sons, Harry and Preston, alone. In 1906, a tornado ripped the roof off the manor, forcing Adelaide and her children to move into the kitchen.

Preston grew up to become a professional boxer, but his career was cut short by a head injury so severe that he was institutionalized. He escaped eight months later in 1935 and returned to Woodlands, where he gunned down his brother Harry in the living room. Harry died in Adelaide's arms. With one son dead and another in prison, Adelaide lost her lifelong desire to restore the family estate to its former grandeur. Before long, the house itself fell victim to the curse. By the time Adelaide died in 1942, Woodland's roofless walls had crumbled, its arches had fallen, and kudzu had enveloped the ruins in leaves and vines.

Barnsley Gardens was finally rescued from forty years of neglect in 1988 when Prince Hubertus Fugger and his wife, Princess Alexandra Bavaria, purchased Barnsley Gardens, which is now home to a luxurious golf resort.

Not surprisingly, the tragic events at Barnsley Gardens appear to have left behind a host of mournful spirits. During the last seven years of her life, Adelaide claimed to have seen her grandmother Julia's ghost strolling the garden and the restless spirit of Colonel Earle when she went to get water from the spring in back of the house. She also heard the laughter of children in a deserted wing, the scraping of her grandfather's chair in the library, and the sound of hammers wielded by ghostly workmen trying to finish Woodlands. Adelaide claimed that her uncle George, who had moved to Brazil years before, appeared to her on the night of his death in South America. In 1941, a week before the Japanese bombing of Pearl Harbor, Adelaide told a syndicated columnist from Atlanta named Colonel Thomas Spencer that the ghost of her son Harry had warned her of the impending attack. All but one of the newspapers that carried Spencer's column deleted it. In recent years, visitors to Barnsley Gardens claim to have seen Harry Saylor's spirit roaming the grounds.

Thanks to the efforts of the new owners, Barnsley Gardens has been partially renovated. Using Barnsley's meticulous letters and records, as well as photographs and plans donated by local residents, Prince Fugger planted 180 varieties of heirloom roses. He also transformed the right wing of the mansion into a museum and landscaped the family graveyard. According to Nancy Roberts in *Georgia Ghosts,* two Cherokee chiefs were invited to Woodlands to remove the old Indian curse that had plagued the old plantation for more than a century. Though the family curse might be gone, it seems that the sad ghosts of the Barnsley family still remain.

The Ghosts of Chickamauga Battlefield

Many years before the arrival of the white man, Native Americans realized that one north Georgia creek was deadly. They called it Chickamauga, or "River of Death," because of the large number of people who drowned there. The creek lived up to its name on September 19–20, 1863, when Union Major General William S. Rosecrans moved his Army of the Cumberland out of northeastern Alabama and northwestern Georgia and headed toward his main objective, Chattanooga. Rosecrans attempted to cut Braxton Bragg's railroad supply line, but with reinforcements from James Longstreet's corps of Lee's army, Bragg's Army of Tennessee delivered a stunning blow to the Army of the Cumberland at the little farming community in the valley of West Chickamauga Creek. Longstreet penetrated the Union Army's right flank, causing a wholesale collapse of the Union line. If Union General George Thomas's left flank had not held firm, the Army of the Cumberland would have been utterly destroyed.

Even though Chickamauga turned out to be the South's last major victory of the Civil War, Bragg's losses were proportionally higher than those of Rosecrans. The Army of Tennessee lost 16,710 killed, wounded, and missing, while the Army of the Cumberland suffered a total of 18,454 casualties. The combined losses of 35,164 men in two days ranks Chickamauga as one of the bloodiest battles of the Civil War. It also is believed to be one of the most haunted of all the Civil War battlefields.

Tragically, not all of the dead or wounded were accounted for. Some fifteen hundred Confederate soldiers and five thousand Federals remained missing in the wake of the battle. After the heavy fog and smoke lifted, wives, mothers, and sweethearts walked among the mangled bodies of the dead and dying, looking for their loved ones. One of these women was a young bride or bride to be, who combed the battlefield in search of her husband. During the day, she gave every soldier she met a description of her lover and inquired as to his whereabouts. At night, she walked over the rocks and through the dense forest with lantern held aloft, looking for her missing beau. She continued to search for him until the day she died. Visitors to the park who are unfamiliar with the legend have seen a woman wearing a white bridal gown roaming through the park. They say her figure is enveloped in a white, shimmering glow.

There are also reports of ghostly soldiers who have made appearances on the battlefield. According to Georgiana C. Kotarski in *Ghosts of the Southern Tennessee Valley,* in 1990, a group of teenagers on a hayride had a terrifying encounter with a spectral rider holding a torch: "As the ghostly green-eyed horse drew near, the group beheld its rider—a skeleton on which a Confederate uniform hung. The gruesome form seemed to dismount, muttering 'Amy, Amy' again and again before finally disappearing."

The most famous of Chickamauga's unquiet spirits is a phantom known as Green Eyes. While a monument was being erected in honor of Opdycke's Tigers, the 125th Ohio Infantry, the widow of an officer killed during the battle donated the emeralds from the earrings he had given her to be used as the eyes of the tiger carved in bas relief. One night, a thief stole the emeralds. People have reported seeing the tiger prowling the park at night when the moon is full, apparently searching for its emerald eyes.

The Watchful Ghost of the 1848 House Restaurant

Marietta's first mayor, John H. Glover, built the mansion he called Bushy Park in 1848. Because he wanted his seventeen-bedroom home to outlast him, he used the finest building materials available at the time: heart pine, hand-forged nails, and locust wood pins. Francis H. McLeod purchased Bushy Park in 1851. The mansion was passed down to his daughter and her husband, Sarah Elizabeth and William King, after McLeod's death.

During the Civil War, a brief skirmish took place on the plantation. Federal and Confederate forces traded gunfire on the property while Sarah Elizabeth and the children and servants huddled in the cellar. After the Battle of Bushy Park, the home served as a hospital for the Union wounded. When he burned Atlanta, General William Tecumseh Sherman refrained from burning down the house because of his friendship with William King. By the time the Union Army left Bushy Park, the house had been stripped of all its fine furnishings. As with many antebellum houses that were transformed into makeshift hospitals, some of the agony and suffering from those tragic times seems to still resonate in Sarah Elizabeth King's beautiful home.

In 1992, the twenty-third owner of Bushy Park, William B. Dunaway, converted the old mansion into the 1848 House Restaurant. Not long after the restaurant opened for business, many of the employees began having some very strange experiences, several of whom Barbara Duffey interviewed in *Angels and Apparitions*. A few of these disturbances seem to have been poltergeist activity. Waiters and waitresses claimed that glasses and furniture seemed to rearrange themselves during the night after the restaurant was closed. Lights in one of the hallway sconces flickered off and on. In the fall of 1995, a hostess and several other employees witnessed a rocking chair on the veranda rocking by itself. Another employee was sitting in a cloakroom when she saw what appeared to be a shadowy, indistinct figure walk up the stairs, down the hall, and vanish into one of the rooms. During the Christmas season that year, a waitress's efforts to create a centerpiece with fruit were frustrated by someone—or something—who kept moving the fruit to different places in the room. Herb Goldstein, headwaiter for seven years, said that he and the other employees frequently detected the odor of a sweet cologne. "It seems to materialize in a huge cloud, and when it appears, all the traffic in that area just stops. All the waiters and waitresses whisper to each other, 'She is here again.' [They] stop for a second to smell the aroma and then just go on about their business." In the late 1990s, employees outside the house saw a woman in a long, white dress standing in a window of the attic, which was used as an operating room during the Civil War.

On October 11, 1998, the Georgia Haunt Hunt Team, a group of paranormal investigators, investigated the 1848 House Restaurant. While the owner of the restaurant was talking to a reporter from television station WSB, one of the group's still cameras captured the image of an orb, which showed up in different locations in several photographs. More orbs were photographed in the attic, which is reported to be the most haunted room in the entire house. One of the most significant images was a strange wisp of light that hovered around the rocking chair, which is said to rock by itself.

In August 2006, the 1848 House Restaurant closed, and the house once again became a private residence. While the house stood empty, people walking around the building peeked into the house and saw a specter, which floated over to a window and adjusted a curtain. Sarah Elizabeth King, it seems, continues to look after her house when no one else will.

The Kennesaw House

In 1855, Dix Fletcher decided to capitalize on the fact that the Western and Atlantic Railroad passed directly through Marietta. He purchased a cotton warehouse that John Glover had built in 1845 directly across from the railroad depot and converted it into a hotel. In no time, the Fletcher House Hotel became one of the finest hotels in Georgia. On April 11, 1862, James Andrews and twenty-one of his Union spies spent the night on the second floor of the Fletcher House. Andrews's raiders planned to steal one of the Western and Atlantic's locomotives, called the General, and blow up bridges and sections of track all the way up to Chattanooga. But unknown to Andrews and his men, they were being pursued by another locomotive, the Texas. By the time Andrews realized that the Texas was right behind the General, it was too late. When the Texas finally caught up with the General just outside Ringgold, all twenty-two men jumped off the train and dispersed. All of Andrews's raiders eventually were apprehended, and Andrews and seven of his men were hanged.

In 1864, General Sherman spared the hotel because Dix Fletcher was a Union sympathizer and his son-in-law Henry Cole was a Union spy. But ashes from other burning buildings ignited the roof of the Fletcher House Hotel, destroying the entire fourth floor. By the end of the war, the hotel had been used as a hospital and morgue by both sides. In 1867, Dix Fletcher reopened his hotel without the fourth floor under a new name, the Kennesaw House. It continued to operate as a hotel until the 1920s, when it became a business office complex. The Kennesaw House was transformed once more in 1979, this time as an office complex. In 1993, the Downtown Marietta Development Authority purchased the old hotel. Then on January 13, 1996, the Marietta Museum of History officially opened on the second floor of the Kennesaw House. Although the curator, Dan Cox, denies the rumors that the Kennesaw House is home to seven hundred spirits, he does admit that he and others have had some very strange experiences inside the old building.

Most of the paranormal activity within the museum is centered in the elevator. In an interview in Barbara Duffey's *Angels and Apparitions,* Cox said that in 1994, he was speaking to his wife in front of the elevator on the second floor, when all of a sudden he realized that a man was standing by the elevator door. The man was about five feet, seven inches tall and wore a flat hat and cream-colored linen overcoat. The apparition's dignified bearing gave Cox the impression that he had been a doctor in life, possibly the nephew of Dix Fletcher, Dr. Wilder. Cox added that the elevator often rises by itself to the second floor, the doors open and close, and then the elevator returns to the first floor.

Cox also believes that he has heard the ghost of the Kennesaw House. He told Nancy Roberts, author of *Georgia Ghosts,* that one afternoon he was talking to two other men in his office, when all three of them heard a tapping noise that began on the first floor and seemed to move upstairs. "It was as if someone wearing a wedding band on their hand was moving along the iron stair rail, their ring clicking rhythmically against the rail while they climbed," Cox said. He left his guests and searched for the source of the strange noise, but to no avail. After resuming his conversation with his guests, Cox heard the noise once again. When he opened the door, the noise stopped. It started up again when he closed the office door. Cox said that this happened a total of four times. Apparently, at least one of the seven hundred ghosts inside the Kennesaw House has a playful streak.

On September 19, 1998, a group of paranormal researchers called the Georgia Haunt Hunt Team investigated the Kennesaw House. By the end of the night, their cameras had captured orbs in a hallway, directly above a portrait in the corner of the ceiling, and on the stairwell. Though the ghost hunters' efforts did not reveal the presence of seven hundred ghosts, they did collect enough evidence to suggest that at least one spirit may be responsible for the unusual occurrences inside the old hotel.

The Wren's Nest

The oldest house museum in Atlanta is the former home of one of the most distinctively southern of all southern writers, Joel Chandler Harris. Following the Civil War, Harris worked as a reporter for the *Macon Telegraph,* the *Savannah Morning News,* and the *New Orleans Crescent Monthly.* In the 1870s, Harris ended up in Atlanta, where he wrote a daily column in the *Atlanta Constitution.* The story goes that one day in 1877, while experiencing writer's block, he decided to write down an African American folk tale that he had heard while working as a printer's apprentice on a plantation. The tale was so popular that he continued to write more. In 1881, Harris included these stories in one of the most popular collections of folklore ever written, *Uncle Remus: His Songs and Sayings.* The popularity of these tales continues to this day. Since the publication of the Uncle Remus stories in 1881, they have never gone out of print. That same year, Harris rented the former home of George Muse, founder of the George Muse Clothing Company. In 1884, Harris hired architect George P. Humphreys to remodel the country house into a one-and-a-half-story family cottage. Another homey touch Harris added to the property was a variety of fruit trees and gardens. When Harris's children discovered that a family of wrens had taken up residence in the mailbox, they made another mailbox for the family mail and dubbed their home the Wren's Nest.

Harris's fifth son, Linton, became very close to his father as the popularity of the Uncle Remus stories increased and allowed Harris to do more of his writing for the newspaper at home. When Linton was seven years old, the boy developed a sore throat. Seven days later, on September 15, 1890, he passed away. For many years, the ghost of a little boy has been seen standing on the stairs in the front hall. Dressed in clothes from the 1890s, he seems to be about seven years old. Evidently, the child is eternally attached to the home where his father regaled him with tales of Br'er Rabbit and Br'er Fox.

On November 11, 2006, six members of the Georgia Ghost Society conducted an investigation at the Wren's Nest. The group arrived at 5 P.M. While the members were seated in a circle in front of the foyer, a loud ringing noise came from the front door. Lane Shakespeare, the curator of the Wren's Nest, said that he had never heard the noise before. When one of the members played back a recording of the ringing sound, it lasted seven seconds, four more seconds than it had lasted before. A couple hours later, Julie Dye, the historical research director, left the group to look for a member named Leanne who had gone to the restroom. As Julie entered the hallway, she saw Leanne standing fifteen feet away, staring into Joel Chandler Harris's daughter's bedroom. When Julie spoke Leanne's name, Leanne jumped and asked, "Weren't you just in the daughter's bedroom?" When Julie told her no, Leanne's face went blank. She said she had seen the tall figure of a woman walking toward the closet. After the group took a ten-minute break, Julie was walking with a male member of the group, Drew, from the tech room to the base of the staircase. While they were walking past the daughter's bedroom, Drew pointed to the mirror and said, "There is a man's face in the mirror." Drew and Julie retraced their steps several times to see if Drew could have seen his own reflection, but he could not because of the angle of the doorway. Later on, Drew and Julie detected a severe drop in temperature in the attic. Both members sensed the presence of children that had been playing up there.

On January 27, 2007, another investigation of the Wren's Nest was conducted by seven members of a Birmingham-based group of investigators called Gulf States Paranormal. Using state-of-the-art equipment, the group got forty-eight hours of video and seventy-eight hours of audio recordings. The members set up eight video cameras throughout the house, one in each room. They illuminated the rooms by resorting to 1970s technology—black lights. Although the group did capture what appeared to be some orbs on film, the director, Cinnamon Tatum, dismissed them as evidence because of the possibility that they may have been nothing more than dust or bugs. Indeed, the seven members of the group likely stirred up a large quantity of dust as they walked on the carpeting. Joel Chandler Harris's room, which has hardly been changed at all since his death, was extremely difficult to film in, because whenever the on-the-floor air vents came on, dust scattered all over the room, thus creating false orbs in the photos. One orb captured on video was interesting, however, because it seemed to move from one room to another.

Several of the members experienced some strange sensations while walking through the house. "In the attic, a couple of people felt dizzy," Cinnamon said. "There is clearly a different atmosphere up there." Cinnamon also felt dizzy and nauseous in the attic, but she thinks it was probably the result of a migraine headache. Undoubtedly, more paranormal investigations of the Wren's Nest will follow.

The Ghostly Doctor of Orna Villa

Orna Villa, the oldest house in Oxford, was built by a Virginian in 1820. Between 1834 and 1837, Dr. Alexander Means bought the house. At the time, he was superintendent of the Manual Labor School near Covington. Between 1838 and 1855, he served as professor of natural science at Emory College, a school that he helped plan in 1837. Dr. Means also lectured on chemistry at the Augusta Medical College, served as president of Southern Masonic College at Covington, and was a preacher in the Methodist church. Between 1854 and 1855, he became the fourth president of Emory College. Not only was Dr. Means a pioneer in scientific education, but he is also said to have demonstrated a workable incandescent bulb in the old Emory laboratory in 1858. A member of many learned societies, Dr. Means died at age eighty-two. The ghost stories that have been circulated about his home for generations reflect his love of learning and a turbulent period in the lives of two of his sons.

An inveterate reader, Dr. Means also stayed up late at night reading the books that he did not have time for during the day. He usually rocked in a rocking chair in his upstairs bedroom while he read. After several hours of reading, Dr. Means kept himself awake by rocking vigorously. For years, many visitors and staff members who have heard the spectral sound of a rocking chair in a long-vacant room attribute the noise to the ghost of Dr. Means, who continues to rock in his chair and read.

Dr. Means had nine children. The most rebellious—and least studious—of his children was Tobe. Dr. Means encouraged Tobe to attend college and become a doctor or lawyer. Tobe, however, wanted nothing to do with higher education. Instead, he wanted to spend the money his father had earmarked for college on a trip abroad so that he could have a "worldly" education. The topic of Tobe's education came up frequently in his conversations with his father, and the outcome was always the same. When Tobe tired of arguing with Dr. Means, he stormed out of the room, slammed the door, and tromped up and down the back porch, all the while decrying his father's obstinate reluctance to really listen to him. One evening, after a particularly bad quarrel with his father, Tobe stormed out of the room, slammed the door, mounted his horse, and rode away, never again to return to Orna Villa. Even today people swear they have heard the sound of someone pacing back and forth across the back porch.

The heavy walking on the back porch could also belong to Tobe's brother Olin, who shared many of their father's characteristics. Unlike Tobe, Olin loved school. He studied medicine, earned his medical degree, and began practicing medicine. Even though Olin was an excellent physician, he began to feel more and more that God was calling him to preach, not heal. In his conversations with Olin, Dr. Means always told his son that only he could decide what God's will was for his life. Kept awake by the stress of having to choose which course his life would take, Olin often walked back and forth across the back porch, mulling over the pros and cons of each career. Before Olin arrived at a final decision, Dr. Means died. Some people believe that Olin, not Tobe, is responsible for the ghostly footsteps heard on the back porch.

In *13 Georgia Ghosts and Jeffrey*, Kathryn Tucker Windham tells of two uncanny occurrences at Orna Villa. In the early 1940s, Mr. and Mrs. E. H. Rheberg purchased the house. They hired a work crew to make specific improvements in the house. One cold morning, Mr. Rheberg woke up just before dawn to look at the plans. While he was reading, he heard someone walking on the back porch. Thinking that one of the workmen had arrived early, he walked back to the porch and looked around. No one was there. The unexplained footsteps ceased after the back porch was enclosed to make a family room. But the next owners of Orna Villa, Mr. and Mrs. John Watterson, often heard doors open and slam shut. One morning, the Wattersons were shocked to find that a collection of guns had fallen off their brackets on the wall and landed on a glass-front bookcase. Incredibly, the bookcase was undamaged. Several framed pictures also fell from the wall, even though they were firmly anchored. Several times, a birdcage fell from its hook in the kitchen. The only explanation Mr. Watterson had was that vibrations from the walking apparitions on the porch had knocked all of these things off the walls. Apparently, Olin's restless spirit has still not made up its mind.

Brenau University's Jilted Spirit

Brenau was founded in 1878 as a liberal arts school for women in Gainesville. The institution has undergone a number of changes over the years. In 1928, Brenau College became the only female college-preparatory residential academy for grades nine through twelve in the state. In 1969, the Evening and Weekend College was established to offer coeducational classes for returning adult students. Like many universities, Brenau is now offering an online college to enable students who are working, traveling, disabled, or geographically isolated to earn a university degree. Brenau University is truly a progressive school, but one element of the past that persists to the present at the institution is the sad story of Agnes Galloway.

In 1926, Agnes Galloway was a first-year piano and voice student at Brenau. The daughter of a prominent family from Mount Airy, North Carolina, Agnes was not nearly as worldly as the other girls at Brenau. She resisted the fashions of the day, preferring instead long, full-skirted muslin dresses. Her old-fashioned innocence contributed to the girl's charm as well as her downfall. She had not been enrolled at Brenau for very long before she fell in love with one of her music professors. One day, while she was playing the piano for him, he placed his hand over hers. Thinking that she had made a mistake, Agnes stopped playing. Her music professor bent over her and kissed her. He then talked to her about destiny. Agnes was so certain that this was his way of proposing to her that she was mortified later on when he announced his engagement to a flapper, the kind of girl who never would have been admitted to a private girls' school. Agnes was so ashamed of being jilted for a common "floozy" that she returned to her room in Pearce Hall, where she slung a rope over a light fixture and hanged herself. The official version of Agnes's death, which the administration presented to the students during an assembly, was that she had suffered a "tragic accident."

Like many legends, the tragic tale of Agnes Galloway has a variant. According to records in Mount Airy, Agnes Galloway died of tuberculosis in 1929, three years after she was supposed to have died at Brenau College. Tammy Pell, a Mount Airy librarian, adds, though, that Agnes's family might have concocted the tuberculosis story to keep their daughter's suicide out of the newspapers and thereby spare themselves any more grief.

Regardless of the true cause of Agnes Galloway's demise, stories of her ghostly return are still passed down by students living in Pearce Hall. In 1996, Nancy Roberts, author of *Georgia Ghosts,* interviewed a junior at Brenau College named Brittany Bell, whose grandmother actually knew Agnes. At the time of the interview, Brittany was living in Agnes Galloway's room in Pearce Hall. She said that one night during a violent thunderstorm, she was awakened by a clap of thunder. Alarmed, Brittany sat straight up in bed. Once she was able to see in the dark, she realized that a girl in a long, white dress with a rope around her neck was standing in the middle of the room. Her grandmother's story of Agnes Galloway's suicide immediately came to mind. A wave of terror swept over the girl, causing her to scream uncontrollably. Several students living on her floor rushed into her room and began reassuring her that Agnes Galloway was not really standing in her room.

The tantalizing legend of Agnes Galloway attracted a group of paranormal investigators to Brenau University on October 30, 2006. Ghost Hounds focused most of its investigation on the auditorium in the first floor of Pearce Hall. In an interview conducted by Mark Davis of the *Atlanta Constitution,* Patrick Burns, the group's director, said he was walking across the stage with his digital recorder, asking questions such as "Agnes, can you talk to us?" and "Agnes, why are you still here?" When he asked the question "Do you want to move on?" he clearly heard someone answer, "What?" A university administrator who was with Burns heard the voice as well. Burns was delighted when he played back his digital recorder and clearly heard the spectral voice say, "What?" After the investigation was over, Burns said that intriguing rumors about the presence of other ghosts in Pearce Hall will probably lead him to conduct another investigation at Brenau University.

Six Flags over Georgia's Ghosts

Six Flags over Georgia is a 230-acre theme park in Austell, just west of Atlanta. It is the second theme park in the Six Flags Theme Parks chain, following Six Flags over Texas, which opened in 1961. When Six Flags over Georgia opened in 1967, it became the first multigate theme park in the United States. It is best known for its roller coasters, four of which were designed by Bolliger and Mabillard. It also installed the first "floorless" free-fall tower ride, Acrophobia, in 2001. Like most theme parks, Six Flags over Georgia has a haunted house, Fearman's Manor, which offers fabricated scares to those guests bold enough to enter. According to many visitors, workers, and ghost hunters, however, the park provides some genuine scares as well.

One of the ghost stories connected with the theme park concerns the Amoco gas station in the parking lot. In the early 1970s, a nine-year-old girl with blond hair was struck and killed in front of the gas station. For years, guests have encountered a little blond girl who runs up to them exclaiming, "Mommy! Mommy! Will you help me find my mommy?" Guests who have walked along with the child to find someone who can help her become panic-stricken when they suddenly notice that the little girl is gone. Usually she disappears after she and the guest have walked ten yards. Some people even claim to have photographed the girl.

Apparently, the Crystal Pistol Music Hall is also haunted. In 1967, shortly after Six Flags over Georgia first opened, an actor remembered today only as Joe was scheduled to appear in the opening number of the first shows ever presented in the theater. Unfortunately, Joe never made the big time; he was killed in an automobile accident on his way to the theme park. Some employees claim that Joe is still hanging around, waiting to go onstage. An apparition has been sighted on several occasions standing on the edge of the balcony, watching the performances. Joe has also been blamed for missing or misplaced props, which sometimes are found near the railroad tracks outside the theater. Ghostly singing emanating from backstage after hours has also been credited to Joe.

The largest number of ghosts at the theme park are said to haunt the Six Flags over Georgia railroad. Passengers on the train have seen several ghosts walking across the Lickskillet Railroad Bridge. Could the apparitions, which are dressed in nineteenth-century western wear and make no noise whatsoever, be the ghosts of actors hired to stage holdups on the train in the late 1960s? Spectators have described them as waiting around for the next train for them to rob.

Jon Waterhouse, writing for *AccessAtlanta* on October 26, 2006, covered an investigation of the Monster Plantation ride by Ghost Hounds paranormal group from Atlanta. One team of investigators walked through the Gotham City section of the park, where Batman the Ride is located. Their digital thermometers registered temperature drops of 30 degrees near the railroad tunnel. They even found a moving cold spot near the Batman ride. Two members of a team assigned to Fearman's Manor became sick. They also recorded two EVPs with their digital recorder: the voice of a little girl saying, "Hip hop," and a woman's voice uttering the name Dorothy. While checking out the Ninja roller coaster and a picnic pavilion, one team member claimed to have been touched by something invisible. Patrick Burns walked through Monster Plantation wearing headphones and holding a digital recorder. He asked a number of standard questions developed by paranormal investigators as a means of collecting EVPs, such as "What's your name?" and "Why are you here?" After a few minutes, Burns played back the tape and was astonished to hear the faint voice of a little girl saying, "Love you." Could the little girl who was killed at the Amoco station still be looking for her mother?

The Apparition at Anthony's Restaurant

Anthony's Restaurant is an arresting sight. Located in Atlanta, which General William Tecumseh Sherman burned on November 15, 1864, the antebellum home that is now one of Atlanta's finest restaurants originally stood in Washington, Georgia, 117 miles east of Atlanta. Wiley Woods Pope started construction on the house in 1797. The second building phase was initiated by Pope's granddaughter Mary Elizabeth Pope Walton and her husband, John Howard Walton. Construction was interrupted by the advent of the Civil War. While John was off fighting for the Southern cause, his pregnant wife remained alone in the house with a young slave girl, Sarah. After Mary's daughter Lulu Belle was born, Sarah nursed the baby. Sherman's troops removed all of the furnishings in the house but refrained from burning it because of the presence of a newborn baby. John was penniless when he returned home from the war, so he was forced to trade the house and all of his property to his father-in-law, Wiley M. Pope. Wiley finished construction on the house and lived there until 1891.

A number of families occupied the home into the early 1900s, but it was abandoned for many years. Then in 1963, an engineer and restaurant owner from Memphis named Dayton Smith undertook the monumental task of moving the house to Atlanta, brick by brick. Smith was so concerned about preserving the historical integrity of the house that he rebuilt it using the original wooden pegs and boards. A banquet hall was added in the 1970s. Unknown to the movers, a female entity might have come along for the ride.

Two names have been suggested for the apparition that haunts Anthony's Restaurant. One of these is Annie Barrett, who was married in the house in 1882 and whose photograph still hangs in the restaurant. Another possibility is the home's last hostess, Annabel, who lived in the house until 1920. After the banquet hall was completed, it was renamed the Ladybug Room in her honor. Employees of the restaurant have been reporting strange occurrences for almost half a century. In an article published in the October 26, 1998, issue of the *Vinings Gazette,* entitled "Atlanta, Georgia's Haunted Restaurant—The Ghost of Annie Barnett," Alan J. Levine said that a chef named Jesse quit his job after seeing an arm emerge from the wall and imitate every movement of Jesse's arm. A former manager of Anthony's, Sally Cwik, said that one night she and her husband turned off the sconces by unscrewing them before they left. As they climbed into their car, they noticed that the sconces on the second floor were back on. Sally believes that another candidate for the ghost could be a woman named Margaret, who worked at Anthony's for thirty years before she died of a heart attack in the back of the house on Valentine's Day. Photographs taken at the spot where she died have registered some eerie anomalies. On September 22, 1998, Levine became the first person to spend the night in Anthony's all alone. Just as he was getting reading to slip into his sleeping bag, Levine heard rapping sounds coming from the ceiling, followed by the tinkling of bells. As he was about to fall asleep, Levine heard someone walking up the stairs. The stranger paused by Levine's sleeping bag and then vanished. Levine experienced this terrifying encounter three times. Not once did he glance at the figure standing beside him.

Several paranormal investigations have been conducted at Anthony's. One of these groups, Ghost Hounds from Atlanta, investigated Anthony's in 2003 with a CNN camera crew. After nightfall, Patrick Burns, the group's director, began interviewing several witnesses. He was sitting on top of the staircase along with one member of the team and two employees of the restaurant. Turning from the witnesses, Patrick began addressing questions to Annabel. After he asked, "Annabel, are you here? Can you give us a sign?" the track lights turned on by themselves. Unfortunately, the cameraman was downstairs and did not film the incident.

Later on, after the CNN cameraman had left, Patrick went downstairs. One of the investigators told him that something weird was happening in the ladies' restroom: "You close the door, and the toilet paper roll in one of the stalls spins around, like a cat would do, playing with it." This phenomenon had been witnessed by Christine, one of the investigators. According to Patrick, "She came running out of the women's room with her pants around her ankles." Patrick then sat in a chair across from the stall. Within four or five seconds, he heard a sound: "dudududududud!" When he and another investigator threw open the door, they were amazed to find three or four feet of toilet paper on the floor.

In 2004, Burns and a single cameraman returned to Anthony's Restaurant, where there was activity that night as well. The most dramatic incident occurred when the cameraman came running down the stairs and said something had reached out and touched him. Neither man should have been surprised. After all, Anthony's Restaurant is renowned for giving its customers the personal touch.

The Haunted Dunwoody House

Atlanta's most famous haunted house was built in 1870 by Jim Donaldson. Donaldson immigrated to Georgia from Great Britain in the mid-1800s, when he was twelve years old, and he grew up to become a farmer. He soon began buying up all the land surrounding his farm at $6 an acre. At the time that he built his dream house, Donaldson bragged that he could walk from Dunwoody to Chamblee without ever leaving his own property. During the Civil War, he served as a captain in the Confederacy. Before he died in 1900, Donaldson married three times and had fourteen children. Births were so frequent in the home that a special room was set aside as a birthing room. He and several relatives who had died of smallpox are buried in a small cemetery behind the house. In 1975, Linda and David Chesnut bought the house, oblivious to the fact that they would not be living alone.

In an interview with author Nancy Roberts in *Georgia Ghosts*, the Chesnuts said that the first indication that something was unusual about their house was the fact that lights seemed to turn off and on by themselves. Their suspicion that something other than faulty wiring might be wrong with the house was validated when David saw a Bible rise up and float in the air by itself. Later on, Linda saw the same thing. A landscaper named Fay Kemp always left before nightfall after hearing a strange noise inside the house. Relatives visiting the house became believers as well when they began hearing the singing of a choir inside the house. People driving by the house reported seeing a woman in a Victorian-style dress staring out the right front bedroom window. David learned later on from descendants of the Donaldson family that that bedroom had been the birthing room. Not long thereafter, Linda saw the apparition herself in the morning while walking into the bedroom. A cousin was the first member of the family to actually see the apparition. She was asleep in bed one night when she woke up to see a lady standing at the foot of her bed, staring at her.

Word of the ghostly activity at the Dunwoody House spread quickly throughout the area. One day a television station expressed an interest in spending Halloween night at the house. The cameraman and a local psychic were walking through the family graveyard when, without warning, the video camera stopped filming. The cameraman was so unnerved that he spent the rest of the night in the van.

The Chesnuts no longer own the Dunwoody House. In an article published by the Cox News Service on February 26, 2006, Charles Yoo reported that the Chesnuts had sold their house to DeKalb County to preserve the house and property from developers. At the time of this writing, the county was still trying to decide whether the house would be used as a community center, museum, or meeting place. Leslie Chesnut, who grew up in the house, never felt threatened by the "strangers" living in the house: "They're just part of the house. They don't seem to want to go on." The Reverend Charlene Hicks, who is also a psychic, was invited by the Chesnuts to walk through the house. She concluded that the spirits are there by choice: "It's not like the spirits are trapped in the house and can't go into the light. They like being there."

The Three Spirits of Bonnie Castle

Bonnie Castle, a five thousand-square-foot brick Victorian house, is a throwback to the golden age of Grantville, back when it was known as a railroad town. Built in 1896, Bonnie Castle was home to wealthy businessman J. W. Colley and his wife, Itura. Soon it became the showplace of Grantville, attracting politicians, preachers, and performers from miles around. President Franklin Delano Roosevelt stayed over at Bonnie Castle on his way to Warm Springs. The Colley family was actively involved in the development of Grantville. Not only were the Colleys successful farmers and bankers, but they also founded the local textile mill. The house was passed down to members of the family until 1981. In 1992, Darwin and Patty Palmer moved into the old house. The next year, they converted Bonnie Castle into a bed-and-breakfast. When the Palmers first started their business, they did not realize that three deceased members of the Colley family apparently were still in the house.

Just a few days after the Palmers moved in, they were awakened in the middle of the night by a loud crashing sound. Exhausted, Darwin and Patty decided to wait until morning to survey the damage. The next day, they combed the entire house, looking for the broken object, but found nothing out of order.

Not long thereafter, the Palmers began to notice a musty smell in the house. Usually the smell appeared at the same time that the Palmers sensed the presence of someone they could not see. One day, when Patty detected the smell in a small space in one of the rooms, she asked the entity, "Is there anything I can help you with?" Almost instantly, the smell was gone. Darwin believed that the musty smell accompanied manifestations of Itura's daughter-in-law Mary. The Palmers also believed it was Mary who turned off the electricity in the entire house one evening when two guests entered her former room.

The only person who has ever seen an apparition in the house is Tess, the three-year-old daughter of a family friend. One day Tess was sitting on the porch steps eating blueberries when she saw someone standing outside the gate. She became very excited and began waving to the stranger, inviting him to come into the yard. Tess's mother, who saw no one at the gate, asked her daughter to describe the man. The little girl said he wore a hat and a yellow shirt. The child's description of the apparition matched a photograph of J. W. Colley, who died in 1898.

In *Haunted Inns of the Southeast,* Sheila Turnage says that the other spirit in the house could be the ghost of Itura. When the Palmers were renovating their home, workmen often complained of being struck by small objects that hurtled across the room. One man was working on a chandelier when a glass figurine flew off the shelf and landed in the middle of the floor. The Palmers theorized that Itura was expressing her displeasure when drastic changes were made in her home.

The Palmers have learned to live with the occasional disturbance in the home. They don't really mind the odd smells or sounds, as long as the ghosts do not bother their guests. Patty believes that Mary and Itura are curious. "They want to make sure whatever we're doing with the house is OK," Patty said.

The Piedmont Hotel

Confederate General James Longstreet, who was born in South Carolina but lived in Georgia, was always a controversial figure. He was promoted to the rank of major general because of his skillful command of the Confederate forces in the first Battle of Bull Run. According to most historians, however, Longstreet did not carry out orders immediately if he did not agree with them. His failure to follow through with his orders led to the inconclusive outcome of the Battle of Seven Pines in 1862. He was blamed for the Confederate loss at Gettysburg, even though he argued against the offensive on the second day of battle.

Following the war, Longstreet angered Southerners by becoming a Republican and accepting posts in President Ulysses S. Grant's administration. In 1875, Longstreet returned to his former home in Gainesville when Grover Cleveland, a Democrat, became president. Longstreet tied his hopes of prosperity to Gainesville's dream of becoming the southeastern railroad hub. He purchased the forty-room Piedmont Hotel and 115 acres just outside town, where he planted vineyards and raised chickens. He also took a position as postmaster.

After his wife of forty years died in 1889, Longstreet started his life over. He married a thirty-four-year-old woman and was appointed commissioner of railroads. In the last years of his life, Longstreet and his second wife rode the rails all over the country. Longstreet died on January 2, 1904, while visiting a daughter in Gainesville. According to some people, Longstreet has never really left the small town that he loved so much.

In *Spirits of the Civil War,* Troy Taylor says that sightings of Longstreet's ghost began in the railroad depot that he visited so often on his trips. He appeared as a man wearing a hat and a white linen duster, standing in the steam of the locomotive. Once the steam had dissipated, the mysterious figure was gone.

Longstreet's spirit has been witnessed in the Piedmont Hotel as well. After the hotel closed down, the building was used as housing for cadets from the Georgia Military Institute. Later, several of Longstreet's descendants lived in the converted hotel. By the 1990s, the portion of the old hotel that remained was being used as a rental duplex. It was acquired by the Longstreet Society in 1994, and renovation of the site began the next year. Since then, a number of workers have reported some very odd occurrences within the old building. One afternoon, a man working in one of the rooms heard someone he thought was his friend down the hallway. He called his friend's name but received no reply. The worker got up and walked toward the doorway. As he passed one of the windows, he noticed his friend standing outside. The two men were the only ones in the building at the time.

Paranormal activity within the building seemed to increase over the next several months. Tools and other items turned up lost, only to appear again the next day in another room. Doors opened and closed by themselves. Some people had the uneasy feeling that someone was standing next to them when they were the only ones present in the room. A number of paranormal researchers believe that the repairs to the house have awakened the spirit of General Longstreet, who is not entirely pleased with the changes being made to his hotel.

Atlanta's Oakland Cemetery

In 1850, the city fathers of the fast-growing city of Atlanta purchased six acres to be used as a cemetery. The burial ground was designed as a rural garden cemetery, which was considered to be a more aesthetically appealing alternative to the traditional graveyard. In 1862, seven of Andrews' Raiders were hanged near the southeast corner of Oakland Cemetery for stealing a Confederate locomotive, the General. After the Civil War, the cemetery expanded to eighty-eight acres, primarily because of the increased demand for burial space by local hospitals where wounded soldiers had died. Extra space was also added for soldiers who had been hastily buried on regional battlefields. By the turn of the century, Oakland Cemetery had become a popular picnic area for local residents. Relatives planted an assortment of gardens in the cemetery to adorn the graves of their loved ones. But it fell prey to vandalism and neglect in the twentieth century. Then in 1976, the Historic Oakland Foundation was set up to stabilize the cemetery. Today Oakland Cemetery is divided into a black section, a Confederate section, a Jewish section, the potter's field, and the original six acres. A number of famous people are buried in Oakland Cemetery, including Margaret Mitchell, author of *Gone with the Wind;* golf legend Bobby Jones; and Maynard Jackson, Atlanta's first African American mayor.

Aside from being Atlanta's oldest cemetery, Oakland is said to be also the city's most haunted. Some of Atlanta's ghost stories are connected to the trees from which the raiders are reputed to have been hanged. In *Ghosts of America's East Coast,* Jackie Behrend quotes from a letter written by a woman to her daughter in 1891. The woman said that she was laying a wreath on the grave of a loved one when she happened to glance up at one of the big trees in the southeast corner of the cemetery. Swinging from a large, overhanging branch was the body of a blue-clad soldier. The gruesome sight immediately brought to mind the story of the Federal raiders who had been executed inside the cemetery.

A Confederate soldier has also been seen inside the cemetery. A young man named Blair Breckinridge told Behrend that he had gone to Oakland Cemetery to place some flowers on his grandfather's grave. As he was leaving the cemetery, he caught sight of something out of the corner of his eye that sent shivers down his spine: A young man dressed in a shabby Confederate uniform was lying directly on a grave, blood oozing from a wound in his chest. Morbid curiosity compelled Blair to walk right up to the prostrate figure. Suddenly the soldier's eyelids opened, revealing not the white orbs of the living, but black, gaping holes. The soldier slowly turned his head and vanished from sight.

Both of the sightings reported by Behrend occurred during daylight hours. One can only wonder what kinds of horrors lurk around Oakland Cemetery at night.

The School Spirits of Young Harris College

A Methodist minister named Artemas Lester first developed the idea of founding a liberal arts school for the residents of Northern Georgia. The college became a reality in 1886 under the name of McTyeire Institute. The college was in danger of closing after its first year of existence, until a judge from Athens, Georgia, Young L. G. Harris, made a generous financial contribution. Harris continued to donate money to the school each year thereafter. Within a few years, the college's name was changed in honor of its first great benefactor. Not long afterward, an act by the Georgia legislature changed the name of the entire village to Young Harris. Today Young Harris College attracts students from places far beyond the Appalachian Mountains. Students from more than a hundred countries have attended the small college. These students return to their homelands with the foundation for a bachelor's degree, Christian sensibilities—and a wealth of ghost stories.

One of the ghost legends circulated around Young Harris College is the story of a janitor known only as Jesse. In the early 1990s, Jesse was assigned to Dobbs Theater, and he soon became a fixture in the theater department. He even played bit parts in some of the college's productions. One evening, as he was headed home, Jesse's car veered off the road and hit a tree. For more than a decade, students and staff have reported paranormal activity, which seems to occur at all hours of the day. At closing time, janitors have turned off all the lights in the building, including the monitor sensor lights, only to find them turned back on when they return the next day. People have heard the sounds of moving chairs in the locked storage room. Footsteps are often heard upstairs and on the catwalk. This is proof, some say, that Jesse will never leave the building he loved so much.

The Clegg Fine Arts Building is also said to be haunted. Supposedly, the ghost of a former president from the 1960s, Charles Clegg, is responsible for disturbances in Clegg Auditorium. Students and staff say that Charlie must have been a frustrated actor in real life, because his ghost sometimes appears onstage and whispers lines to actors. He has also been known to play the organ. People who do not realize that Charlie is a kindly spirit recoil in horror when they feel the cold touch of dead fingers on an arm.

Students living in the dormitory have created a ghost legend of their own. They say that the recently constructed dormitory sits on the place where a student with a poetic soul hanged himself years ago. Today his ghost resides on the second and third floors, where he causes the blinds and closet doors to shake and computer monitors to turn off and on by themselves. Students have also heard spectral knocks on their doors and noises emanating from an empty bathroom. The student's ghost has also been seen reading poetry on the lawn and hanging from the ceiling. Telling stories of the student's ghost has become an informal part of the orientation for freshman residents of the dorm.

The Worcester House

The Worcester House is the only original building remaining in the reconstructed Cherokee Indian village of New Echota. New Echota, Cherokee for "New Town," was officially designated the capital of the Cherokee nation on November 12, 1825. In 1828, a young missionary named Samuel Worcester built the two-story house that bears his name. He continued to live and work with the Cherokees until 1832, when Georgia's Sixth Land Lottery gave away the Cherokee land to settlers. That same year, Worcester was arrested and sentenced to four years' hard labor because he and eleven other missionaries had published a resolution protesting a law prohibiting all white men from living on Indian land without a license. In 1833, the new governor, Wilson Lumpkin, released Worcester and another missionary, Elizur Butler, from prison after forcing them to agree to minor concessions. The next year, Worcester and his family were forced to move from their home because it had been purchased by a man who had obtained title to the house in the 1832 land lottery. Worcester and his family moved to Oklahoma with a number of Cherokees to await the arrival of the rest of the Cherokee nation. By 1838, seventeen thousand Cherokees had been forced to leave Georgia and walk eight hundred miles west on what is now known as the Trail of Tears.

The entire town of New Echota was abandoned for more than a century, with the exception of the Worcester House, where a number of families have lived over the years. On March 13, 1957, the state of Georgia reconstructed New Echota as a state park. The Worcester House, which had stood empty for two years, was fully restored. People say that the tragic history of the Cherokees and the whites who have occupied the Worcester House is imprinted within the very walls of the old house.

A number of violent acts were perpetrated in the Worcester House. In the 1830s, two Cherokees were playing cards in a room downstairs. One man accused the other of cheating, and a fight ensued. Both men wound up dead on the floor. Newspaper articles dating as far back as 1889 recorded a number of paranormal disturbances within the Worcester House. People have reported hearing the rattling of chains. One man who lived in the house said that the floor downstairs "stayed bloody all the time." The floor was replaced years ago. The ghost of a thin, gaunt man has also been seen in the house. Gary Green, curator at the Worcester House, is fairly certain that this is not the spirit of Samuel Worcester because he was a short man. Green is very familiar with some of the more recent disturbances in the house: "Objects seem to move by themselves, like a spinning wheel whose wheel has been seen turning on its own. I was here with a lady who works part-time on the weekends, and both of us saw a rocking chair on the porch rock by itself. It was a windy day, but the rocking chair was sitting across the direction of the wind, so it couldn't have been the wind that moved it." Green also said that people have heard disembodied footsteps walking up and down the stairs. "Three years ago, we had the inside of the house painted. One day, the painters left an old man here by himself. I warned him that the house gets weird sometimes, but he laughed and said he wasn't worried. A couple of days later, the painters came back, and they told me that the man they'd left behind said he heard footsteps. He searched the entire house and didn't find anybody. He told us that he wasn't going to work there by himself anymore." Green speculated that the old painter probably wouldn't laugh again if someone told him that the Worcester House was haunted.

The Georgia Bigfoot

No one north of the Mason-Dixon line really thought of the South as the stomping ground of Bigfoot until the 1972 film *Legend of Boggy Creek* focused the spotlight on the Fouke Creek Swamp Monster in Arkansas. It should come as no surprise, therefore, that there have been fifty Bigfoot sightings in Georgia, most of them occurring in the northern part of the state. Many of these Bigfoot encounters have been posted on the Georgia Bigfoot website, georgiabigfoot.com. In an article entitled "Tales of Bigfoot Legend Include Sightings in Georgia—Even Clarke County," Wayne Ford wrote about a hair-raising experience Jack Hovatter had while hunting in the forests of Fort Gordon Army base when he found a large humanoid footprint near Elkins Creek. Curiosity drove him back to the area a week later. He was taking a path leading toward the creek when he saw an apelike creature, ten feet tall, about fifteen feet ahead of him. Its face was somewhat similar to that of a gorilla. Cautiously, he backed out of the thicket.

In another article entitled "Elkins Creek Revisited," Sam Rich, who runs the Georgia Bigfoot website, detailed the history of what has come to be known as the Elkins Cast. In 1997, a police officer named James Akin was investigating a series of disturbances at a mobile home. The owner, identified only as Mr. W, complained that someone had been hitting the side of his trailer in the middle of the night. He said that the intruder made a huffing sound as he followed Mr. W's movements inside the trailer. As the man was talking, Akin became aware of a pungent smell permeating the air. He also took note of a fifty-pound sack of dog food that had been ripped apart. Thinking that someone might actually be harassing the man, Akin walked around the trailer, looking for tracks. He made his way over to a muddy little island in the middle of Elkins Creek and was amazed by what he found: two seventeen-and-a-half-inch-long footprints, the largest he had ever seen. Even though Akin suspected that the prints might be a hoax, he made a plaster cast of the better of the two prints. Later the cast was examined by Dr. Jeff Meldrum and forensic fingerprint expert J. H. Chilcutt. Both men concluded that the footprint was real. Interestingly enough, the disturbances on Mr. W's property ceased shortly after the track was cast. Akin assumed that whatever had made the print moved on.

In 2005, Alex McRae wrote about a recent Bigfoot-type sighting in north Coweta County. Donna Robards told McRae that on August 22, her eighteen-year-old son Jeff was on his way back to Happy Valley after dropping off his sister in her east Coweta home. Jeff was approaching the intersection of Cedar Creek and Happy Valley Roads when he saw an apelike animal walking down the middle of Cedar Creek Road, straight toward his car. He was so startled by the two-legged creature that he drove off as fast as he could. Three days later, Donna drove to the same intersection to verify her son's story. Just before reaching the intersection, Donna came to a screeching stop to avoid hitting not one, but two apelike creatures, one eight feet tall and the other seven feet tall. One of them ran off into the woods; the other one started walking toward Donna's car but then took off after his companion. She never again doubted her son after the events of that horrifying night.

The Public House Restaurant's Spectral Lovers

The Public House Restaurant is one of the oldest buildings in Roswell. Built in 1854, the Public House was originally the commissary for the Roswell Mill, which is located directly behind the restaurant. The mill, which manufactured cotton, thread, and woolen goods, paid its workers in scrip that could be redeemed only at the commissary. Because the commissary charged inflated prices for its goods, the workers soon found themselves in serious debt. During the Civil War, when food and clothing were needed for the war effort, workers were forced to barter for the necessities of life with their meager possessions and crops they had grown in their gardens. In 1864, General William T. Sherman saved the Public House from destruction so that it could be used as a hospital for the Union wounded.

After the Civil War, the upstairs floor was used as a funeral home. One can still see the hole in the ceiling through which caskets were raised and lowered. In the 1920s, a small section of the building, which was partitioned off by brick columns, housed the Dunwoody Shoe Shop. For more than twenty-five years, the building has housed a gourmet restaurant. The Public House's bare brick walls, hardwood floors, and fine cuisine have attracted customers from Roswell, neighboring Atlanta, and beyond. Of course, the romantic ghost story connected to the old building is a plus for ghost enthusiasts.

For years, waiters and waitresses have regaled customers with the story of two ill-fated lovers who lived in Roswell during the Civil War. Katherine was a sixteen-year-old girl who worked at the commissary. One July day in 1864, a seventeen-year-old soldier named Michael, who was attached to Sherman's army, caught the girl's eye when he stopped by the store and paid cash for his purchases. Before long, the couple began stealing away to the upstairs loft for a few moments of privacy late in the evening after Katherine closed the store. One day, Michael made an excuse to talk to Katherine outside the store. Hiding behind a tree several yards away from the long line of people standing outside the store, Michael warned Katherine that within a day, Federal troops would close down the mill and commissary and arrest the workers on the charge of aiding and abetting the Confederate Army. He begged Katherine to run away with him and hide with his relatives in the mountains until the Confederate Army finally surrendered. Then they could get married. Their fate has been left up to local storytellers. Some say that Michael was eventually wounded and died in the building. Others say that Michael was killed in battle and never returned to Katherine. The more romantically inclined believe that they traveled to one of the Northern states and were married.

Regardless of which version of the lovers' fate one accepts, the general consensus among the staff at the Old Public House is that their spirits have returned. Waitresses who set the tables the night before have returned the next morning and found that the napkins, silverware, and plates on a table in a corner have been moved around, just as if a couple had eaten there the night before. The most active area in the restaurant is the loft where the piano bar is located. One morning, two chairs that had been pushed against a table the night before were found placed in front of a window. In *Ghost Stories of Georgia,* Chris Wangler says that one night, two sisters were drinking cognac in the darkened room when they began hearing footsteps coming from the other side of the room. Knowing that they were the only customers up there that night, the women assumed that members of the staff were doing some cleaning. After a few minutes, the sound of the footsteps was replaced with whispering. One of the women addressed the shadowy figures but received no reply. The sisters returned to the restaurant and told the hostess about the strange sounds in the piano bar. She told the women that they were definitely the only ones up there.

In October 2005, a group of paranormal investigators called Historic Ghost Watch spent the night at the Public House Restaurant. One of the investigators felt something tug on her dress. Two other members of the group "chased" something in the restaurant by tracking sporadic 2.0 readings on their electromagnetic field (EMF) detectors. EVP included such words as "All right," "Ed," and "Get in here." The group concluded that the restaurant was definitely "paranormally active," but they could not prove that it was haunted.

Gaithers Plantation

Preserving historic 155-year-old Gaithers Plantation has become a labor of love for the residents of Covington. The Friends of Gaithers Plantation raise money by giving tours of the two-hundred-acre estate. One volunteer who enjoys dressing up in period clothing and giving tours is Judy Dial, whose maiden name is Gaither. Her genetic connection to the family who built the plantation house might explain why one of the spirits stopped by the bridal room one day when she was changing clothes. Judy says that all at once the door opened and the doorknob jiggled, but no one was there. Visitors have seen figures dressed in mid-nineteenth-century attire standing in windows of rooms that were supposed to be empty. One day a visitor saw a man wearing the uniform of a Confederate soldier standing in the basement. Volunteers believe this could be the spirit of one of the Confederate soldiers who hid out in the home during the Civil War.

Several teams of paranormal investigators have spent the night in the old house. One of these groups, the Georgia Ghost Society, captured a red, firelike image in a photograph taken in an upstairs bedroom. When Andrew Calder, the photographer, magnified the image, he was surprised to see the figure of a woman to the right and behind the fire, which appears to be a candlestick. A photograph taken in an upstairs bedroom by codirector Drew Hester revealed a white fog or mist hovering around a window. Not coincidentally, this is the very room where a number of people have seen the spectral lady.

Beware of the Wog

At first glance, Winder is just another sleepy, little Georgia town. According to Native Americans, however, this region was once home to a monstrous creature called the Wog. This legendary beast, which was said to be a long-haired, jet black animal, was as large as a small horse. Its hind legs were much shorter than its front legs. The monster's most distinctive feature was its tail, at the end of which was a fanlike tuft of white hair that the Wog kept in a constant up-and-down motion. The resulting whizzing sound could be heard twenty-five or thirty steps away. From its bearlike head darted a forked tongue, said to be at least a foot long. The Wog's fearsome appearance was enhanced by its red eyes and great white teeth that protruded over its closed lips. This nocturnal creature stalked settlements at night in search of small animals, such as dogs and cats. Early settlers claimed that they could see the forked tongue poking through the chinks in their log cabins.

The Creek Indians believed that the Wog was the Devil. He lived in Nodoroc, a mud volcano that was the Creek version of hell. The Creeks threw condemned criminals and prisoners into the boiling mud of Nodoroc, where they were thought to be consumed by the Wog. According to one Creek legend, Chief Umausauga had a beautiful daughter, who rejected the advances of a Choctaw suitor. The spurned warrior killed the young woman and fled into the forest. Days later, the girl's father and brother caught up with the warrior and killed him. They then cut out his heart and fed it to the wolves. The Creeks carried his body to Nodoroc and threw it into the boiling pit to be consumed by the Wog. Hungry for revenge, the Creeks swore vengeance on the Choctaw, but every war party was repelled by the Wog, who scared the braves to death and then ate their bodies.

The Wog appears again in the tale of a woman named Fenceruga, who murdered and ate one of her children. Chief Urocasca dispatched a hunting party with orders to capture her and bring her back to Nodoroc, where she was thrown headfirst into the boiling

lake. Her body struck the mud with such force that it made a deep impression, which roused the sleeping Wog. The Wog was so startled that he rolled over and over again in the mud and began sweeping his tail back and forth. For years, reports circulated concerning a screaming woman who ran over the hills on dark nights, pursued by an army of laughing children. Who knows what it will take to awaken the Wog once again?

Savannah

SAVANNAH'S STORIED PAST DATES BACK CENTURIES BEFORE JAMES
Oglethorpe brought over the first boatload of settlers on September
11, 1732. Shell middens, or mounds, indicate that Native Americans inhabited this site as far back as 3000 B.C. The city is built
over the burial sites of the earliest inhabitants, whose mounds were
leveled in the eighteenth century to make room for the city's first
buildings. As Savannah grew, the site of the city's first real cemetery on the southwest corner of Wright Square was paved over. The
Jewish burial ground was developed as well; at least sixteen bodies
lie between the east- and westbound lanes of one of Savannah's
main streets. In 1927, a work crew laying storm drains on Gordon
Lane unearthed several skeletons from a slave burial ground in full
view of a group of schoolchildren. To this day, road crews and util-
ity companies occasionally exhume the bodies of the city's earliest
settlers. Savannah is truly a city built upon its dead.

Savannah can also be said to be a city that has passed through a
trial by fire. Very few eighteenth-century structures still exist in
Savannah because of the fire of 1796, which destroyed more than
300 houses. The great fire of 1820 was even worse, claiming 463
buildings. The next major fire, Hogan's fire of 1889, began at
Hogan's Store on Broughton and Bernard Streets. Ironically, Savannah's fires proved to be a boon to architects and builders, as well as
to doctors and undertakers.

Even more death and destruction were heaped upon Savannah during the Civil War. After the fall of Fort Pulaski on April 10, 1862, a total blockade of Savannah was put in place. As a result, inflation ran rampant. Food was expensive and in short supply. By 1865, most of the men and boys in the city were gone. Many families in Savannah had lost loved ones. The misery produced by the Civil War and the other calamities that have beset the city has left an indelible impression on the psychic fabric of Savannah.

Fort Pulaski

Fort Pulaski was Robert E. Lee's first military assignment. He was assigned the task of draining the swamp on the site where the fort is now located in 1831. No expense was spared to make the fort impregnable. Twenty five million bricks, handmade at the Hermitage Plantation on the Savannah River, went into its construction. When Pulaski was completed eighteen years later, the fortification was considered state of the art. But although the fort was protected with fifty cannons and masonry walls seven and a half feet thick, it proved to be no match for rifled cannon fire. Union forces under the command of Captain Quincy A. Gillmore began the bombardment of Fort Pulaski on April 10, 1862. The experimental guns easily drilled through the southeast scarp of the fort within hours. Before Gillmore's artillery could hit the powder magazine, Colonel Charles H. Olmstead surrendered thirty hours later, at 2 P.M. The fall of Fort Pulaski signaled the end of the era of masonry forts. Two years later, the fort became a prison for six hundred Confederate officers, who subsisted on starvation rations in deplorable living conditions. Thirteen of the forty-four men who died there are buried within or around the fort. Since 1933, Fort Pulaski has been owned by the National Park Service. The park contains 5,365 acres, including some of Georgia's most pristine marshland. According to eyewitnesses, Fort Pulaski contains a few ghosts as well.

Sightings at the old fort began soon after it was designated a national park. According to Margaret Wayt DeBolt in *Savannah Spectres and Other Strange Tales,* an unidentified woman told her that during World War II, she was returning from Tybee Island when she spotted several soldiers walking along the parapet of Fort

Pulaski. At the time, the fort had been taken over by the Navy, so she was uncertain which century the soldiers belonged to. During the same time period, a young soldier from Hunter Field was walking the perimeter of the fort with a friend when they detected the sound of footsteps coming from the other side of a clump of bushes. The footsteps were moving in the same direction the two young men were. As they walked along, they began noticing that the tall marsh grass was being mashed down, as if someone were walking through it. The frightened young men raced to shore and hastily clambered aboard their boat. A psychic told DeBolt that as he descended the stairway leading from the ramparts, he was overcome with an oppressive sense of sorrow and misery. Later she found out that a soldier who had been mortally wounded during the bombardment of Fort Pulaski in 1862 had died as he was being carried down the stairs.

More recently, James Caskey reports in *Haunted Savannah* that a couple told him they were passing by the fort at dusk when they saw a soldier pacing across the top of one of the walls. He was wearing a dark uniform, reminiscent of the dark gray uniforms favored by some Confederate soldiers. Another man who was walking into the powder magazine heard a voice say, "Charlie, come here." The man was the only person in the powder magazine. Perhaps there is some truth to General Douglas MacArthur's belief that "old soldiers never die; they just fade away."

Fort McAllister

Unlike Fort Pulaski, Fort McAllister was far from being a state-of-the-art fortification. Constructed in 1861 by engineer John McGrady just below Savannah, Fort McAllister was surrounded by massive earthen walls, which were designed to absorb the impact of cannon balls. Within the protective walls of the fort were a hospital, barracks, and powder magazines. The fort also boasted a ten-inch mortar battery. Fort McAllister's defenders heard the sound of battle for the first time on July 1, 1862, when the Union gunboat *Potomska* opened fire on the fort. The ship backed off when it became clear that it was outgunned by the fort's artillery. On July 29, 1862, Fort McAllister came under Union attack for the second time when a Confederate blockade runner, *Nashville,* sought refuge in the waters around the fort. Union ships pursuing the *Nashville* fired their cannons at the fort, only to have their cannon balls "swallowed up" by the earthen ramparts. On January 27, 1863, the fort was bombarded by the USS *Montauk,* a Federal ironclad. Neither the fort nor the ironclad sustained any significant damage, so the *Montauk* attacked Fort McAllister again on February 1. Both sides traded volleys, with the same result as the first time. The 230 Confederate troops defending the fort were finally overrun by 4,000 of General Sherman's troops on December 13, 1864. A number of park officials and tourists believe that some of the long-dead Confederate soldiers are still manning the old fort.

After the Civil War, Fort McAllister was all but forgotten. Vines, bushes, and trees reclaimed much of the land. In the 1930s, automobile magnate Henry Ford, the owner of the property at the time, began restoring the fort. Fort McAllister was not completely restored until the area was acquired by the International Paper Company, however, which deeded it to the state of Georgia. Fort McAllister was open to the public in 1963.

Reports of unearthly activity at Fort McAllister emerged during the restoration process. According to Dave Goodwin in his online article "Fort McAllister: The Phantom Feline of the Savannah River Defenses," a number of the men hired by Ford in the 1930s to work on the fort refused to spend the night there because eerie noises kept them awake. To this day, some visitors tell park officials that they heard strange sounds within the fort.

Two of the ghosts in the park have reportedly materialized. One of these is the spirit of the fort's commander, Major John B. Gallie. During the seven-day assault of Fort McAllister, a Union ironclad and several wooden ships began firing at the Columbiad, a huge cannon placed on one of the fort's earthen mounds. One of these shells ricocheted off the parapet, striking Major Gallie directly in the head. Some eyewitnesses said that the shell scalped the heroic major, exposing his brains; other swore that he was completely decapitated. In *Banshees, Bugles, and Belles: True Ghost Stories of Georgia,* Barbara Duffey says that one February morning in the 1960s, around the anniversary of Gallie's death, several of the groundskeepers were cutting the grass around the Columbiad when they saw a headless figure standing on the exact spot where Major Gallie had been killed, looking out to the river. The man was dressed in a dark blue militia uniform, the style used by officers until gray uniforms were available.

An inhuman spirit also makes an occasional appearance in the fort. Camp mascots, such as dogs and cats, were common among many units during the Civil War. Fort McAllister's mascot was a black cat named Tom Cat. He was adored by all of the soldiers at the fort, even though black cats have been traditionally believed to bring bad luck. Tom Cat enjoyed running back and forth along the grassy embankment, even during bombardments. The feline's luck finally ran out on March 3, 1863, when he was struck by a stray round. Tom Cat was so beloved by the men that following the attack on the fort, he was listed as the only casualty in a report sent to General Beauregard. It seems that the ghost of the mascot has haunted the fort for decades. Tom Cat's spirit is still seen running through the fort and over the earthworks. Some people have even reported feeling an invisible presence rubbing against their legs. A plaque erected to Tom Cat's memory is a testament to the soldiers' affection for the feline. Tom Cat's periodic visits to the fort reflect his everlasting love for the only home he ever knew.

Wright Square

Some of the earliest arrivals to Savannah were indentured servants. These were people who did not have money for the passage to America and got someone to sponsor them. They were then required to work for this person for four to seven years.

In December 1733, forty Irish servants arrived in Savannah, one of whom was Alice Riley. She and another servant named Richard White were placed in the household of William Wise, whose job it was to look after the trustee's cattle. Wise had been unable to tend to the cattle because of a recent illness, so Alice and Richard were assigned to assist him until he recovered sufficiently to do the job himself. Wise had long, white hair that hung down to his waist. One of Alice's daily chores was to go down to the river, bring back buckets of water, dump them into a large tub, and bathe Wise. She then washed his hair, combed it out, and plucked his beard.

One March day in 1734, after some particularly outrageous behavior by Wise, Alice and Richard held his head in the bucket and drowned him. The couple fled but were captured two days later and put on trial. Even though there were mitigating circumstances relating to the old man's cruel and malicious behavior, Alice and Richard (who some sources say were married) were found guilty and sentenced to death.

After the sentencing, everyone in the audience walked over to Wright Square and watched the hanging of Richard White. His body was left hanging for three days. Alice was brought out, kicking and screaming, right after Richard's execution. Just before the noose was placed around her neck, she announced, "I'm pregnant." Alice was returned to jail, where she sat for eight months. After the baby was born, it was put up for adoption. Despite the authorities' reticence about executing a woman, Alice was hanged in Wright Square under the cover of darkness. The height of the gallows was doubled so that her body would not be as visible from the ground. Alice Riley and Richard White were the first people to be executed in the colony of Georgia.

The tragic tale of Alice Riley has given rise to a host of ghost stories. According to the oldest of these legends, Alice's corpse was left hanging all night long. When the magistrate and jailer returned the next morning to cut her body down, they were surprised to find that her body and the hangman's rope were missing. One of the men pointed out that every single scrap of Spanish moss in the tree was gone as well. Some residents of Savannah believe that Alice has been condemned by God to pluck every scrap of Spanish moss from these trees for eternity, just like she had to pluck William Wise's beard.

Some people also say that the ghost of Alice Riley is still searching for her baby around Wright Square. In April 2005, Linda Davig and her daughter had a very unnerving experience in the square: "We were leaving the square when my daughter heard footsteps behind her. She stopped and turned around but saw nothing. As I turned around and looked at her, she started to advance toward me when we heard the footsteps again. She stopped and turned around, but again, nothing was there. She continued walking. Then all of a sudden, something came up and hit her backpack. She turned around and took a picture anyway. In her backpack was my purse and other things. She looked at me and said, 'Mom, that woman— something hit my backpack, and I'm really upset.' I said, 'Nobody stole my purse?' She said, 'No, there was no one there. Something hit my backpack, and I believe it was that woman, looking for her baby.'" When Linda looked at the photograph her daughter had taken, she was not surprised to see an orb in front of one of the trees in Wright Square. "The orb was big and round. It was also white and transparent," Linda said. The women's experience has convinced them that the love of a mother for her child transcends death itself.

The Moon River Brewing Company

One of the best reasons for visiting Savannah is the unique cuisine offered in its period-flavored restaurants. One of these fine eateries is the Moon River Brewing Company, which is just as renowned for its great beer as it is for its excellent food. The restaurant's hospitality is undoubtedly a holdover from its past. The building in which the Moon River Brewing Company is housed was originally the City Hotel.

Construction on the hotel began in 1819, but work proceeded slowly because of fines and a fire that damaged the unfinished building. Undaunted, Elazer and Jane Early continued with the project. When the City Hotel finally opened in 1821, it was also home to the Bank of the United States and the postal service. A number of famous people stayed at the City Hotel in the nineteenth century, including War of 1812 hero Winfield Scott, the Marquis de Lafayette, the first three commodores of the U.S. Navy, and John James Audubon, who lived at the hotel for six months while he finished work on his book *Ornithological Biographies.* In 1851, new owner Peter Wiltberger renovated the hotel and even put a lion and lioness on display. The City Hotel closed in 1864 with the arrival of General William T. Sherman's army, but it reopened at the turn of the century as a coal and lumber warehouse. When coal was no longer an important energy source, the building was used for general storage. In the 1960s, the City Hotel's next incarnation was as an office supply store, which closed in 1979 when Hurricane David struck Savannah and blew off the roof. The building was abandoned until renovations began in 1975. On April 10, 1999, the Moon River Brewing Company opened its doors on the site of the former hotel. The most enduring remnants from the building's past are not the ornate columns and balustrades, but the ghosts who refuse to check out.

The Moon River Brewing Company's most famous ghost story has its origins in one of the feuds that often broke out among the politicians and businessmen who frequented the bar in the City Hotel to drink and talk. One evening in the spring of 1832, a drunken, belligerent man named James Stark expressed his hatred for a local doctor, Philip Minis. Dr. Minis initially took Stark's insults as nothing more than the ravings of a fool whose anger was fueled by alcohol. When Stark accused the doctor of cowardice, however, Minis had had enough. On August 10, James Stark and a friend were walking down the stairs of the City Hotel just as Dr. Minis declared, in a loud voice, that James Stark was a coward. As Stark reached in his pocket, Dr. Minis drew his gun and killed Stark. The judge pronounced the murder of James Stark justifiable homicide, and Dr. Philip Minis went on to a distinguished career as a U.S. Army surgeon.

In recent years, the Moon River Brewing Company has become as well known for its ghosts as it has for its fine food and service. Most of the violent paranormal activity within the restaurant is attributed to the vengeful ghost of James Stark. Some employees and customers have felt as if someone were pushing them down the stairs. A female apparition has also been seen in the old hotel, looking out the window facing Bay Street and descending the stairs.

Poltergeist activity has been reported at the restaurant as well. In an article in the October 11, 2005, edition of the *Clarion Ledger*, reporter Russ Bynum said that the basement seems to be the focus of many of the disturbances. Candles placed on tables in the basement have relit themselves twenty minutes after being blown out. One day just before closing, a worker saw a hooded figure standing in the darkness. On one occasion, a folding chair that had been propped up against a window righted itself and opened its legs. Witnesses have seen silverware move by itself on empty tables. Investigations conducted by at least two ghost-hunting groups since 2005 have collected enough evidence to suggest that the Moon River Brewing Company could indeed be haunted. But the people who work there were convinced long before the paranormal investigators showed up.

The Haunted Orphanage

Throughout much of the eighteenth century, Savannah was a beleaguered city, beset by war, fire, and yellow fever. The secondary casualties of these calamities were the children who were left without homes or parents to care for them. As a response to this need, a boys' orphanage was opened in 1740. There was no refuge for female children until 1820, however, when a girls' orphanage was opened on 117 Houston Street. It was operated by a Baptist minister named Henry Cunningham. The girls who lived in this small house were well fed and cared for. Then in 1827, tragedy struck. A fire broke out in the orphanage. Rescuers thought they had removed all of the girls from the house until they did a head count and realized that two of the girls were missing. A spectator gazing up at the top of the house saw two girls frantically trying to escape from an attic window. One of the rescuers tried to go back into the house, but the smoke was too heavy. Tragically, the two little girls died in the fire. Their mischievous spirits are still said to be the only orphans left in the former girls' orphanage.

The ghosts of the girls who died in the fire have appeared to many of the people who have owned and lived in the house over the years. The girls are usually dressed in period nightgowns with shawls draped over their shoulders. On one occasion, a policeman was called to the square by a concerned citizen who feared that the little girls' mother was neglecting them. For many years, neighbors have seen two little girls in nightgowns frolicking in Green Square. In *Savannah's Ghosts,* Al Cobb says that one night, a friend of one of the owners of the house awoke to find two little girls standing at the foot of his bed. A few years later, a boy living in the house saw two little blond girls dressed in their nightgowns at 3 P.M. Additional visual evidence has taken the form of small handprints that have appeared on the attic windowpanes. Efforts to wipe off the handprints have usually proven futile, because they always return.

Much of the poltergeistlike activity that has been reported inside the house could be construed as the playful antics of the two little girls. Inanimate objects such as spoons seem to move by themselves. Sometimes objects such as cell phones vanish from one location and mysteriously reappear in a different room. Visitors to the house have noticed a distinct drop in temperature in the kitchen

and at the foot of the staircase. Lights turn on and off by themselves. The most recent owners said that they always turn the television off before they leave the house, but sometimes they find that it has been turned on when they return home. Incidents such as these have helped cement the house's reputation as one of the most active paranormal sites in Savannah.

The Isaiah Davenport House

Visiting Savannah is like taking a trip back in time, thanks largely to the preservation efforts of the Savannah Foundation, which is responsible for saving about 750 of the city's historic buildings. One of the foundation's first successes was the Isaiah Davenport House, which was spared in 1955 just before it was slated to be destroyed by the wrecking ball. A master builder from Rhode Island named Isaiah Davenport built the house in 1820 as a residence for himself, his wife, and their six sons and one daughter. The Davenport House is now a house museum that attracts thousands of tourists a year, many of whom are anxious to see the house that served as the model for the MacKay home in Eugenia Price's novel *Savannah*. But for some tourists, their visit to the old house has been more like a journey to the other side.

Many visitors have noticed a large Persian cat poking its nose around the corner of the building as they approach the entrance to the gift shop. When they open the door, the cat runs into the gift shop ahead of them. As the visitors are paying for their purchases, they ask the cashier about the cat. The cashier laughs and informs them that a cat has not lived in the house since it was opened as a museum in 1955.

The cat is not the only occupant who makes periodic appearances. Several years ago, a Victorian toy exhibit was put on display in the Davenport House. Near dusk, two ladies who had been walking around upstairs went down to the gift shop and noticed that the cashier was getting ready to close up. One of them asked the cashier, "What about the little girl upstairs?" The cashier replied, "There is no little girl upstairs." The lady was insistent: "Yes, there is. She is playing in one of the rooms with the toys." Concerned that the child had become separated from one of the tours, the cashier accompanied the ladies upstairs. A quick inspection of all the upstairs rooms produced no little girls. Puzzled, the ladies exited the gift shop. While they were walking to their car, one of the ladies looked back and was startled to see a little girl looking down at her from the middle window. They learned later on that many people have seen a little blond girl in a white Victorian lace dress standing at that window. She has also been seen sitting in the rocking chair upstairs.

The little girl is believed to be the ghost of Laura Davenport, who ran down the stairs one day after playing with her dolls and tripped and fell. She went into a coma, from which she never emerged. Laura now haunts the upstairs rooms of her beloved home, locked in eternal childhood, with no companions but her fluffy cat.

The Olde Pink House

The Olde Pink House is one of the finest examples of eighteenth-century Georgian architecture in all of Savannah. It was built in 1771 on Abercorn Street by James Habersham Sr., a merchant, politician, and planter. He was also an ardent supporter of King George III. He had ten children, but only three sons survived into adulthood. James was alternately proud and ashamed of his eldest son, James Habersham Jr., who made a fortune in rice and shipping but arranged for the Sons of Liberty to hold secret meetings in his father's house. Later James and his brother John served in the Continental Army, fighting against what they perceived to be the tyranny of the British Crown. Death finally resolved the differences that kept James Sr. and his sons apart: All three were laid to rest together in Colonial Cemetery.

In 1812, Habersham's house became the Planter's Bank. During the War of 1812, gold captured from the British was stored in one of the bank's two vaults. Fifty-two years later, the bulding served as the headquarters for Brigadier General Lewis York following General William T. Sherman's March to the Sea. For the next hundred years, Habersham's home was transformed into a law office, a tea-room, and a bookstore. At some point, the house was covered in stucco, which turned pink periodically from the red brick underneath. In the 1920s, the lady who ran the tearoom painted it pink. In 1971, on the home's two hundredth anniversary, Herschel

McCallar Jr. and Jeffrey Keith opened a restaurant and Colonial tavern inside the old residence. The bank vault was converted into a wine cellar, and the parlor is now a dining room—reasons enough, some say, for the ghost of James Habersham Sr. to disturb the tranquility of the Olde Pinke House.

The strange occurrences in the Olde Pink House have attracted the attention of newspaper reporters and writers for years. The old house has even been featured in the Travel Channel program *America's Most Haunted Places: Savannah*. Workers claim that furniture has moved around during the night when they open the restaurant. The door to the ladies' room has been known to lock and unlock itself. Customers walking outside the house have looked through the dining-room window and seen people walking around in the candlelight. According to James Caskey in *Haunted Savannah*, one of the waitresses was trying to remove a tablecloth from a table when she felt something tugging on the other end. Another waitress blew out the tea lights in the dining room, only to find that some of them had rekindled themselves after she left the room. On another occasion, a waitress followed a figure dressed in the attire of an eighteenth-century serving girl up the stairs and into the north dining room but found no trace of her when she walked inside. Nancy Roberts reports in *Georgia Ghosts* that one night after the restaurant had closed, a number of employees were on the first floor when they saw the door to the second floor open and a misty shape ascend the stairs.

James Habersham Jr.'s ghost has been seen as well, usually in one of the rooms upstairs. In *Ghost Stories of Georgia*, Chris Wangler says that in 2001, a customer who had finished his meal asked to be guided around the historic structure. While they were walking around upstairs, the tour guide was called downstairs, so the customer continued touring the upstairs on his own. As he walked down the hall, he noticed a man wearing eighteenth-century clothes and a powdered wig. Thinking that the man was an actor, he said hello. The strange man said nothing, so the customer complimented him on his costume. The man's repeated refusal to answer made the customer so uneasy that he ran down the stairs. While he was looking for his guide, he recognized a familiar face in a portrait hanging in the foyer. It was a likeness of James Habersham Jr., the same man he had seen upstairs, who apparently is still the master of his house.

The Pirate's House

The name of the Pirate's House restaurant is somewhat misleading. Though it is true that the tavern was frequented by sailors in the eighteenth and nineteenth centuries, it is unlikely that very many actual pirates stopped by for a drink. The Pirate's House was built in the Old Fort area only a few feet from the Savannah River between 1753 and 1794. By 1730, most of the pirates in the area had been driven out by the Royal Navy. But there might be some truth to the legend that Robert Louis Stevenson wrote much of his pirate novel *Treasure Island* in the old tavern.

Even though most of the stories about pirate activity in the restaurant are apocryphal, the Pirate's House is deserving of its nefarious reputation. Drunken brawls often resulted in one or both of the combatants being stabbed or shot. Many unsuspecting sailors were plied with alcohol, carried through a tunnel leading to the river, and shanghaied aboard strange vessels en route to parts unknown. In the twentieth century, the Pirate's House was operated as a house museum until it was purchased by the Savannah Gas Company. The wife of the gas company president, Mrs. Hansell Hillyer, converted the old tavern into one of Savannah's most popular restaurants, renowned for its fine cuisine—and its ghostly past.

Former owner Herb Traub said that one night just before closing, the night manager walked into his office. Visibly agitated, he told Traub that after he had finished closing up one of the restaurant's fifteen dining rooms, he was walking down the hall and glanced into another room, where he saw a strange-looking man sitting at a table. The night manager had paused a moment to collect his thoughts, then walked back to the room and looked in again. The strange man was gone.

A number of ghost stories revolve around the secret tunnel. Sealed for many years, the tunnel begins in the brick cellar beneath the Captain's Room. A number of employees claim to have heard spectral voices emanating from this part of the cellar. Another legend that has been passed down for many years in Savannah concerns a young man who was so fascinated by the stories about the secret tunnel that he decided to explore it himself. He was making his way through the tunnel when he tripped on something round and hard. He dug around the stonelike object and was shocked to find that he had uncovered a human skull. The young man gasped and dropped the grisly relic. Undaunted, he continued walking through the tunnel until a pile of rubble blocked his way. Suddenly he heard a group of men walking behind him. He pressed himself against the wall and held his breath as five men dressed in pirates' clothes walked past him and through the mound of rocks and dirt that had blocked his way. At that moment, the young man was convinced that he had seen enough. He ran back through the tunnel as fast as he could go.

Apparently, the kitchen is haunted as well. James Caskey says in *Haunted Savannah* that a cook was working alone in the kitchen one night when a man dressed like a nineteenth-century sailor walked right past him and through the door. The cook was so shaken that he never again worked alone in the kitchen at night. He also wore a large crucifix as insurance against the ghosts of the Pirate's House. The Pirate's House, it seems, still belongs to the pirates.

The William Kehoe House

The William Kehoe House is unique for reasons that are not readily apparent to the casual observer. When William Kehoe, the owner of an iron foundry, built his Queen Anne style mansion in 1892, he protected it from the recurring fires in the city with an iron framework. Even the exterior ornamentation is made of iron. William and his wife had ten children. After Kehoe died, his wife lived in the house for many years. Between 1910 and 1975, the home served as a funeral home. In 1992, the present owner spent $1 million renovating the house. Today the Kehoe House is the only four-star bed-and-breakfast in Savannah. It is also one of the most haunted hostels in the entire city.

A record of many of the sightings in the house can be found in the guest book. The night concierge has placed a red star by the names of all the guests who have had a paranormal experience during their stay. Two ladies wrote by their names, "Stay in Room 201 if you want to see a ghost." Room 201 is usually one of the last rooms to be rented out because it has two single beds. Most people who stay in this room experience the same phenomena. Guests sitting on the bed or in a chair watching television have felt someone rub them lightly on the back of the head or touch them on the cheek. During October Fest 2002, a woman was in Room 201 alone while her husband walked down to Bay Street to watch the fireworks display. She began feeling sick, so she lay down on the bed. Suddenly she heard a knock on the door. Standing outside the door were two children, a little girl and boy. The little girl said to the woman, "We're scared." The woman told her that the booming noise was caused by the fireworks and there was nothing to fear. She shut the door and returned to bed. The next morning, she asked the innkeeper about the little boy and girl who had knocked on her door the night before, and he said that no children had stayed at the hotel for at least three weeks.

Another strange encounter in Room 201 occurred in December 2002. A couple from Ohio had just returned from shopping and eating lunch at Claire's at 2 P.M. Exhausted, they decided to lie down for a short nap. While her husband was in the restroom, the woman felt someone sitting at the head of the bed. She opened her eyes and saw a little blond girl sitting on the bed. At first she thought it was her daughter, but then she remembered that the child was staying in Ohio with relatives. At this moment, her husband walked out of the bathroom, and he saw the little girl too. The couple stared at each other in disbelief, just long enough for the little girl to disappear.

The best-known ghost is a lady in white who roams the halls and rooms of the house. It is said to be the ghost of Mrs. Kehoe, whose spirit is restless because her body was transported to the Catholic cemetery in a wagon instead of a hearse, as she had requested. In August 2000, the night concierge was walking down the stairs to the linen closet in the basement. As she reached the bottom step, she was overcome with a feeling of dread. Goosebumps rose on her arms. She stepped into the hallway, turned around, and saw the translucent shade of a woman hovering a foot above the ground. The night concierge was frozen in fear. She began rocking back and forth, unable to look at the apparition. Finally she said a prayer: "God, please let her go away." She looked up, and the woman was gone.

James Caskey reports in *Haunted Savannah* that another employee had an unnerving experience in the hotel several years ago when she was sitting at the front desk, reading. All at once, the front doorbell rang. She looked through the glass window in the door and saw no one standing outside, so she returned to her reading. Thinking that there was problem with the wiring, she paid no attention when the doorbell rang a second and a third time. After the doorbell rang a third time, the door opened all by itself. The young woman became even more frightened when she discovered that all of the outside doors in the house had been opened. Not everyone who works at the Kehoe House has seen the ghosts, but those who have encountered the spirits have never been the same since.

The Owens-Thomas House

The Owens-Thomas House on Oglethorpe Square has been called the most beautiful house in Savannah. It was designed by British architect William Jay for a relative of his by marriage, a wealthy cotton broker named Richard Richardson. Richardson's wife, Frances, died in 1822, only three years after construction on his house was completed. Richard lived in the house alone until he lost it in a financial depression. In the 1820s, the home was converted into an upscale boardinghouse run by Mary Maxwell. Its most famous guest was the Marquis de Lafayette, who stayed there in 1825. The house was purchased by Congressman George Owens in 1830, and members of the Owens family occupied the home for more than a century. The last member of the Owens family, Margaret Thomas, died in the house in 1949, and it became a house museum a year later. The bed in which Margaret died is still there, and according to stories told by employees and visitors, so are some of her ancestors.

In *Savannah Spectres and Other Strange Tales*, Margaret Wayt DeBolt says that a maid has had some strange experiences in the house. On more than one occasion, she made sure that everything was in perfect order in the dining room before locking up for the night. When she returned in the morning, she found that one chair had been pushed away from the table, as if someone had just left the dining room after eating a hearty meal. On another occasion, she found a puddle of water on the floor, several feet away from any plumbing or windows.

Other people have had odd experiences in the house as well. For many years, people walking past the house at night heard the sounds of a piano playing inside. On more than one occasion, Margaret

Thomas, who often wore a long, old-fashioned gown and shawl while walking around the garden, was mistaken for a ghost.

Savannah antique dealer Jim Williams, who later achieved national notoriety as the pivotal character in the book *Midnight in the Garden of Good and Evil*, claimed to have had an actual encounter in the house in the 1960s, when he was sharing a drink in the front room with his business partner and a friend who was renting the entire upper floor of the Owens-Thomas House. Jim and his business partner were sitting in two single chairs; their host was sitting in a two-seat couch facing them. They had been talking for an hour when Jim's business partner noticed that a man had materialized in the back of the room behind the couch where their host was seated. Jim described him as an equestrian of the nineteenth century. The apparition wore a short-waisted coat and tall, black riding boots. He held a riding crop in his right hand. Jim and his business partner watched the ghost walk around the back of the room for ten minutes, but their host saw nothing at all. Then, without warning, the ghost walked through the two-seated couch and stood over Jim. His face was so close to Jim's that the antique dealer could see his blue eyes. For a moment, Jim turned toward his business partner, who was visibly shaken. Jim looked back at the ghostly figure, and he was gone. Jim said he was so close to the man that he could see beads of sweat on the man's forehead. Later Jim joked that Savannah got so hot in the summer months that even the ghosts perspired.

A week later, the man who was renting the upper floor was walking up the center staircase when he saw a man walking down the stairs, dressed exactly as Jim Williams had described. Frantically, he ran back to the front door and drove to the Hilton Hotel, where he spent the night. The man moved out of the Owens-Thomas House shortly thereafter, convinced that the entire time he lived there, he was never really alone.

The Hampton Lillibridge House

Hampton Lillibridge based the design of his home on East Bryan Street on his memories of his Rhode Island boyhood. Built in 1796, the house is one of the few homes to survive the great fire of 1820, when 463 homes were destroyed. For the next century and a half, the house went through several owners and eventually was converted into a tenement house. By the time eccentric antique dealer Jim Williams purchased the old house, it had stood vacant for several years. He moved it to its present location at 507 East Julian Street in 1963, during the height of Savannah's restoration movement. The restoration process had just gotten started when Jim, a noted believer in the occult and paramormal, realized he had bought much more than he had bargained for.

Despite the Hampton Lillibridge House's charming appearance, it had a violent past that seems to have lingered on into the present. It is said that when it was a tenement house, a sailor hanged himself from the knob of a high brass headboard in one of the bedrooms. Memories of this incident were resurrected when the house was being moved. The house next to the Hampton Lillibridge fell on one of the workmen and killed him. Once the restoration process actually began, brick masons reported hearing people walking and whispering upstairs. Jim went to the house to check out the rumors, and he too heard the strange noises upstairs. He walked upstairs and was relieved to find nothing up there. He assured the brick masons that the house was empty, and they returned to work. The next day, however, the spectral footsteps and talking resumed, and the brick masons refused to come back. In desperation, Jim asked the Episcopal bishop, the Right Reverend Albert Rhett Stewart, to perform an exorcism. Reverend Stewart asked the spirits to leave and blessed the house.

Convinced that the house was "clean," Jim asked the workmen to return to work. One man who was working late had just finished varnishing the upper floor and walked down the stairs when he heard someone running around on the floor above him. The exasperated workman dashed up the stairs, expecting to find his freshly varnished floor ruined. Instead, he found no evidence that anyone had been upstairs in his absence. The floor was completely unmarred.

When Jim finally moved into the house in May 1964, the workmen made bets as to how long he would be able to stay in the house by himself. Shortly after moving in, Jim was lying in bed asleep. All of a sudden, he felt that he was not alone in the upstairs bedroom and woke up. His suspicions that he was not alone in the house were confirmed by the sound of someone running down the hallway. Jim pursued the intruder to the staircase but saw no one downstairs. A few weeks later, three of Jim's friends occupied the house in his absence. They were sleeping downstairs when they heard someone moving around upstairs. One man went upstairs to investigate. After a few minutes, his friends went upstairs to check on him and were alarmed to find him lying on the floor facedown. He told them that as he had crossed the floor, he began to feel as if he were walking in freezing water. Suddenly something grabbed him and dragged him toward the unfinished chimney shaft. He blacked out after that.

By this time, Jim realized that he needed advice from an expert on the paranormal. Nancy Roberts says in *Georgia Ghosts* that Jim contacted William G. Roll of the American Psychical Research Foundation. Roll spent four days alone in the house, looking for natural explanations for the phenomena, such as underground lakes or caverns. Roll concluded that the paranormal activity was generated by "human waves" produced by human beings after undergoing a traumatic experience. Roll called the Hampton Lillibridge House "the most psychically possessed house in the nation."

Most of the people who have lived in the Hampton Lillibridge House since Jim Williams have been reluctant to discuss their experiences in order to protect their privacy. In *Haunted Savannah,* James Caskey reports that one of the recent owners had trouble keeping babysitters or maids. On one occasion, a door downstairs was found pried open from the inside. To this day, passersby have seen a woman dressed in Victorian-era clothing pacing around the widow's walk. One evening, neighbors called police to complain about a loud party going on inside the Hampton Lillibridge House. When the police arrived, they found the house completely empty. The owners, it turns out, were out of town at the time.

Jim Williams revealed his theory about the hauntings to Margaret DeBolt. He said that while workmen were digging the foundation for the house at its new location, they uncovered an underground crypt, half filled with water but empty of its original occupant. Could it be that the occupant of the crypt is expressing his displeasure at being evicted from his resting place?

The Juliette Gordon Lowe House

The ghost story connected with the Juliette Gordon Lowe House demonstrates that not all ghost stories are tragic, melancholy, or frightening. For many years, Girl Scouts have made pilgrimages to the birthplace of their founder, Juliette Gordon, totally unaware of the house's romantic past. It was built for Judge Moore Wayne, an associate justice of the Supreme Court, in 1820. After Judge Wayne left for Washington, his nephew William Gordon bought the house.

In 1858, William moved his bride, Nellie Kinzie, into the mansion. Nellie was so attached to William that when he left Savannah to fight for the Southern cause, she traveled to Virginia and asked General Robert E. Lee to help find her husband. After Savannah fell to Union forces, General William T. Sherman personally delivered mail and candy to Nellie and her children. He also allowed her to leave with a flag of truce for South Carolina. Nellie and William returned to their Savannah home in 1865. William stayed by Nellie's side until duty called him away once more, this time to serve in the Spanish-American War as a brigadier general. After the war, Presidents William McKinley and William Howard Taft paid tribute to William Gordon. All of Savannah mourned William's passing in 1912, but no one mourned more than Nellie. She never concealed the fact that she loved William even more than her own children and longed to be united with him in death.

Nellie got her wish on February 22, 1917. Her five children and her daughter-in-law, Margaret, were keeping a deathwatch in the house. Margaret had just said good-bye to the dying woman and was awaiting the inevitable in an adjoining bedroom when she saw William Gordon, dressed in his gray suit, walk out of Nellie's bedroom. After Nellie died, the butler told Margaret and her husband, Arthur, that he had seen William leave the bedroom, walk down the stairs, and exit through the door. Upon returning to Nellie's bedroom, Margaret was struck by the smile on the old lady's face, which was strikingly similar to William's cheerful expression.

The spectral presence that occupies the Juliette Gordon Lowe House today behaves more like a poltergeist. The spirit seems to be attracted to "newfangled" objects, such as ballpoint pens, calculators, or staplers. Staff members arriving in the morning have found sheaths of paper stapled together. Sometimes objects disappear for three to five days, and then mysteriously reappear on a table in a corner of the room with the lamp on. Occasionally a worker has asked the ghost, "Please bring back my calculator." Then the next day, the object appears on the table with the lamp. Apparently the ghost of the Juliette Gordon Lowe House enjoys taunting the people who work there.

The Marshall House Hotel

Built in 1852 by Mary Marshall, the daughter of a cabinetmaker, the Marshall House was originally a hotel. In 1857, Mary added the hotel's trademark cast-iron balconies and veranda. It was used as a Union hospital during the Civil War and two of Savannah's yellow fever epidemics. In 1867, it briefly housed the volunteer Fire Department. The hotel attracted celebrities from all over the South, including Joel Chandler Harris, who lived there briefly while working as a post-Civil War editor for the *Savannah Morning News.* Around the turn of the century, Minnie Geiger took over the hotel and renamed it the Geiger Hotel, after herself. In 1933, ownership of the hotel changed again. For the next twelve years, the hotel was leased to Herbert W. Gilbert. The hotel closed in 1945 but reopened a year later as the Marshall Hotel. After the owner's ten-year lease ran out in 1956, the hotel closed once again, seemingly for good. Then in 1999, after a $12 million renovation, the 150-year-old hotel reopened once again, this time as the Marshall House Hotel. It is now one of the most luxurious—and most haunted—hotels in Savannah.

Staff members and guests suspected that the Marshall House Hotel was haunted from the very beginning. James Caskey says in *Haunted Savannah* that shortly before the hotel's grand opening in August 1999, the staff noticed strange odors emanating from Rooms 214, 314, and 414. When deodorizers and group prayer failed to dispel the odor, the staff turned on a radio that was tuned to a gospel music station. The smell disappeared soon thereafter. Not long after the hotel opened, guests reported hearing childish laughter and children's footsteps running down the hallway. They also heard the sound of a ball bouncing down the stairs. One night, a sleeping guest felt the sensation of having his feet tickled. He woke up with a start and was surprised to see a little girl standing there. As he stared at her, the child smiled and vanished before his eyes. Other guests have felt hands pressed against their foreheads while they were asleep, just as doctors and nurses would have done when the hotel was used as a Union hospital.

One of the possible causes for the haunting of the Marshall House Hotel was uncovered while the hotel was being remodeled in the late 1990s. Workers were removing some rotten floorboards in a downstairs office when they founded several batches of human bones. Because this room served as an operating room in the winter of 1864, staff members have surmised that after surgeons amputated the mangled limbs of Union soldiers, they stashed the remains under the floor. Hidden away for 135 years, the grisly souvenirs of the Civil War slowly decomposed. As soon as the bones were removed, employees began hearing strange noises inside the office. According to Caskey, a night manager working in this downstairs office caught a glimpse of one of these patients, who wore a blue uniform and was missing an arm. Another night manager was working in the office when someone—or something—began reorganizing her stacks of documents and money. In 2005, a night manager was working late one night when a padlock on one of the cabinets began swinging by itself, making a clacking noise. When she could no longer stand the irritating sound, she asked the ghost to stop playing with the lock. The lock immediately stopped moving. The same young woman has felt a cat rubbing her leg while she sat at the desk. Every time she has reached down to pet the feline, the cat disappears. Employees will tell you that all of the apparitions in the Marshall House Hotel are friendly, even the animal ghosts.

The Hamilton Turner Inn

The Hamilton Turner Inn was originally built as a home by Samuel P. Hamilton in 1873. A former blockade runner during the Civil War, Hamilton became a jeweler and president of the electric company, and his personal fortune was one of the largest in Savannah. Eventually Hamilton became mayor of Savannah. As a result of Hamilton's wealth and social status, his house became one of the social centers of Savannah. It was one of the first houses in Savannah to have electricity. He also filled his home with objets d'art from all over the world. To protect his collection from burglars, Hamilton hired a sentry to stand guard on the roof. One morning, when the sentry did not show up for breakfast, a servant climbed the stairs to the roof and found the sentry lying in a pool of blood. He had been shot, apparently by an intruder. Hamilton himself stood watch atop his house for a while, but ill health forced him to abandon his post. Hamilton died in 1899. Even though the Hamilton Turner Inn did not serve as the model for the Haunted Mansion at Disney World, as has been rumored, the old house does have its share of ghosts.

Hamilton's parties attracted dignitaries from all over the country. During these lavish affairs, Hamilton's five children, four boys and a girl, were restricted to their bedrooms or to the play area upstairs, where they played pool. Instead of making themselves scarce while their parents were entertaining, the children amused themselves by rolling billiard balls down the stairs. When the children were really bored, they threw the balls at their parents' guests. It is said that one unfortunate target received a billiard ball on his head.

When Nancy Hillis bought the house in 1991 and began renovating it, she discovered that the Hamilton children were still misbehaving. She told Sheila Turnage, author of *Haunted Inns of the Southeast,* that she distinctly heard the sounds of children giggling. She also said that a tour guide heard pool balls bouncing down the stairs one evening. A lady who was working in the gift shop said that late one afternoon, she saw a yellow ball rolling down the stairs. The child ghosts have also been known to lock themselves inside their rooms on occasion.

Apparitions have been sighted in the old mansion as well. Nancy Hillis said that tour guides have seen the milky form of a man in the house. Guests have reported seeing the ghostly shape of a man having a heart attack, just as Hamilton did in 1899. They have also seen an authoritative-looking man in a Victorian-era suit sitting in a chair at the top of the stairs. Hillis and a tenant also heard the sound of a large man running up the stairs one night. She called the police, but they were unable to find the intruder. According to Nancy Roberts in *Georgia Ghosts,* a woman who worked in a shop across the street told her that one moonlit night, she saw a man standing on top of the roof. She stared at the figure for a few moments, until a cloud blocked out the moon. After the cloud passed away, the figure was gone. It seems that someone—possibly the sentry or Samuel P. Hamilton himself—is still protecting the Hamilton Turner Inn.

The Telfair Art Museum

The Telfair Art Museum was originally a home designed by architect William Jay in 1818. Mary Telfair, whose father was a former governor of Georgia, lived in the house with her sister Margaret Hodgson and brother-in-law William Hope Hodgson until her death in 1875. Mary willed her opulent mansion to the Georgia Historical Society to be used as an art museum. Her will stipulated that the Telfair Art Museum and Hodgson Hall, which was under construction at the time of her death, would have "no eating, drinking, smoking, or amusements of any kind." After the museum had its formal opening in 1886, the consequences of defying her will became painfully clear.

It has always been understood that Mary Telfair did not want her huge oil portrait removed, although she did not express this request in writing. In the mid-1980s, workmen temporarily removed her portrait from the dining room. Immediately, part of the rotunda fell through the lower ceiling beneath it.

Margaret Wayt DeBolt says in *Savannah Spectres and Other Strange Tales* that the consequences of violating the conditions of Mary's will are even more severe. A few years ago, a meeting of the Georgia Historical Society was held on the lawn behind Hodgson Hall. Without warning, black storm clouds began forming overhead. Within minutes, the sky opened up; soon the ground was littered with tree limbs and hail the size of golf balls. All of the tables and refreshments were moved inside to escape the storm's fury.

Suddenly a gust of wind blew through the building, causing a glass to fall and break on the floor. Some guests claimed that they heard voices in the wind. After this terrifying display of nature's—and Mary Telfair's—wrath, refreshments are served only in the newly constructed annex.

More recently, a caretaker at the Telfair Art Museum discovered for himself that Mary Telfair still keeps a constant eye on her former home. Chris Wangler says in *Ghost Stories of Georgia* that the caretaker was in the habit of "taking a nip" now and then from one of the bottles hidden in a closet and was shocked to find that all of his liquor bottles were gone. He was baffled because he was the only one who had a key to the closet. As he was leaving the building, he slipped on a wet spot on the floor. The caretaker was certain that the floor had been dry before he left. Other people claim to have heard phantom footsteps and the lilting tones of a harp in the Telfair Art Museum. It seems that not even death can prevent Mary Telfair from keeping watch over her beautiful home.

The 17Hundred90 Inn and Restaurant

The 17Hundred90 Inn was constructed around 1820 on top of the foundations of an older building that was probably built in the 1790s. The first owner of the Federal-style building was Steel White, a prominent Savannah merchant, who had just married Anna Matthewes Guerard. The ghost legends connected with the old inn have made it just as popular with paranormal researchers as it is with lovers of good food and drink.

Two female ghosts are said to haunt the 17Hundred90 Inn and Restaurant. Diane Greenfield Smith, a former owner of the inn, told Margaret Wayt DeBolt that one of the ghosts is the spirit of a black cook with a fondness for large bracelets, who worked in the kitchen in the 1850s. Smith described the ghost as a vehement spirit that cannot tolerate the presence of another woman in her kitchen. The former owner was in the kitchen one day when she heard the jangling of bracelets and felt someone give her a hard push. One morning, the concierge was walking through the kitchen when one of the serving trays on top of the refrigerator fell at her feet. The trays had been stacked one inside the other, making it difficult for a single tray to fall. Some of the kitchen help have seen knives and spoons fly off the table.

But the 17Hundred90 Inn and Restaurant is best known for harboring the spirit of an Irish servant girl named Anna Powers, who, according to one legend, fell in love with a sailor who may or may not have been married. He shipped on boats transporting cotton from Savannah to England. Following one trip to England, Anna's lover failed to return, so she threw herself off the third-floor balcony into the brick courtyard. In another version of the tale, Steel White imported Anna as a child bride from Ireland and held her prisoner in Room 204 while he prepared for their wedding. A few days before the nuptials, Anna jumped off the balcony and killed herself. Other versions of the fate of Anna Powers are also told around Savannah.

Whatever really happened at the old inn, it seems that the psychic residue of a terrible tragedy still resonates within its walls. At times, guests have found their clothes laid out for them on the bed. As a rule, the staff credits Anna with this "random act of kindness." Once a guest said that she had laid her undergarments on a chair before stepping out for the night. When she returned, her undergarments were gone. One family saw the form of a young girl wearing a long dress sitting in a chair on the portico. Other people have seen rocking chairs rocking by themselves and windows opening on their own. In the 1990s, a concierge took a bottle of wine to Room 106. Usually the door does not shut all the way, but she had just set the bottle on the dresser when the door slammed shut. One night, a waitress was serving iced tea to a group of three young men and three young women. After she set the tray on the table, one of the glasses exploded. The waitress said that this sort of thing often happens when a beautiful woman is present.

Most of the haunted activity in the 17Hundred90 Inn and Restaurant takes place in Room 204. A man staying in the room was awakened by drops of water falling on his head. The concierge had a plumber check out the room and found nothing wrong. Later the man likened the water drops to tears. On several occasions, the telephone in Room 204 has rung late at night, but no one was there. The telephone company said that it would be impossible for the phone to ring in Room 204 without passing through the switchboard first. In 2002, the foreman of a work crew was changing a showerhead when he heard voices in the bedroom. He walked over to the bed and found no one there. While he was standing there, scratching his head, the television came on by itself. He found out later that guests had complained about hearing loud talking while they were asleep.

Some of the other rooms on the second floor apparently are haunted as well. Rena Harp, director of Foothills Paranormal Investigations, was staying in Room 203 with her friend Tammy in 2005. They had returned from a ghost tour at 3 A.M. Just for fun, they decided to get out their pendulum to see if their room was haunted.

After a few moments, the pendulum began swinging furiously back and forth. Rena took a photograph of the pendulum and was amazed at what she saw: "It was a skull with eyes and nose, and you could see its tongue sticking out. It is quite amazing!" Before the women checked out of the 17Hundred90 Inn and Restaurant, a maid told the women that just ten minutes before they arrived, a woman had run screaming out of Room 201. They checked out shortly thereafter. Anna, it seems, still cannot tolerate the presence of another woman in the only home she had during her short stay in Savannah.

Southern Georgia

SOUTHERN GEORGIA IS COMPOSED OF TWO LAND REGIONS. THE ATLANTIC Coastal Plain, which covers more than a fourth of the state in the southeast, is noteworthy for its sandy loam soil, ideal for growing tobacco, watermelons, and peanuts. At the southern part of the Atlantic Coastal Plain is Okefenokee Swamp, a marshy, tropical wilderness that is forty miles long and thirty miles wide. The East Gulf Coastal Plain, which spreads across the southwestern part of Georgia, has even more fertile land.

Southern Georgia is definitely one of the most mysterious areas in the entire state. Stories of ghost lights, river monsters, giant hogs, poltergeists, UFOs, and centuries-old curses are still told around campfires and in college dorms. Some parts of Southern Georgia are just as wild and forbidding as they were before the railroads brought with them settlers and civilization. As long as swamp gas, deep shadowy forests, and the eerie cries of birds and beasts continue to stimulate the imagination, Southern Georgia will continue to be a hotbed for weird tales for generations to come.

The Screven Light

At one time, Screven was the largest town in Wayne County because of its association with the railroad. Screven became a railroad town after a trestle was built over the Altamaha River at Doctortown in 1857. After the Atlantic Coast Line Railroad Company (ACL) located its rice yard in Waycross, Screven's population began to decline.

Today, Screven is known as the site of the Screven Light. The legend of a flagman who was struck by a train as he was swinging his lantern has been passed down in town for generations. People have been seeing the light ever since the Civil War. For years, churches brought hayrides to the railroad tracks at Milligan's Crossing to await the coming of the light. Although rational explanations for the phenomenon, such as swamp gas, have been around for years, hundreds of people still flock to the railroad tracks in hopes of catching a glimpse of the Screven Light.

In *Georgia Ghosts,* Nancy Roberts tells the story of a carload of high school kids who drove out to Milligan's Crossing one night. They parked their car and gazed down the tracks toward Jessup. Suddenly they saw a faint glow in the distance, moving down the railroad tracks in their direction. The girls and boys got out of the car and stood by the tracks to get a better look. As the glow of the light intensified, the girls screamed and climbed back into the car. The light then passed over their car and vanished into the darkness. One of the girls described the light as a white, glimmering ball that swung from side to side as it passed down the tracks.

The Cogdell Light

The little town of Cogdell promotes itself as the home of actor Ossie Davis, who was born there on December 18, 1917. But Cogdell is probably better known for a strange light that has been seen bobbing along the fringes of Okefenokee Swamp between Cogdell and Waycross for more than a century. One of the legends generated by this phenomenon is similar to the one connected to the Screven Light. Late one night, a railroad man was decapitated by a passing train. He now prowls the swamp with a headlight, looking for his missing head. In *Ghost Stories of Georgia,* Chris Wangler describes an encounter Ed Jordan and his girlfriend Cathleen Dupree had with the headless specter one night in August 1999 in Okefenokee Swamp around Waycross. The figure appeared to be a little shorter than average size.

Another legend has it that in 1861, the owner of a large plantation enlisted in the Confederate Army. Thinking that the war would be over in a few weeks, he told a servant to wait for him every night with a lantern at the crossroads. When his master failed to return after two weeks, the servant remained at his post, holding his lantern. For three decades, the servant waited for his master. Finally, in the 1890s, he died. The plantation is long gone, but the glow of the servant's lantern is still visible as he awaits his master's return.

Surrency's Spook Light

Surrency, a sleepy little town of three hundred people, was incorporated in 1911 along the Macon-Brunswick railroad tracks. At its peak in the 1920s, Surrency was recognized as the "crosstie center of the world" with as many as five carloads shipped out each day. These days, Surrency is much better known for its ghost light, sightings of which date back to the turn of the century. Most locals describe it as a bright yellow ball that vanishes when people get too close. In an article on the Surrency Spook Light appearing in the online *Rowlett Report*, Curt Rowlett describes a conversation he had with an eyewitness, James Joyner, from nearby Baxley. Joyner told Rowlett that one night, he was standing on the train track with some friends when he sighted "a very bright, golden-yellow light about the size of a grapefruit" hovering over the railway. As Joyner slowly made his way down the track, the light swiftly flew toward him and disappeared, only to reappear behind him.

Those looking for a rational explanation for the phenomenon theorize that the "ghost light" could be a product of an ancient reservoir of water or some other fluid nine miles under the earth. Most of the residents of Surrency, however, believe that the light is connected to the town's most famous nineteenth-century attraction, the Surrency Ghost.

The Surrency Ghost

The Surrency Ghost supposedly haunted the house once owned by the town's founding family. The ghost first appeared in 1872 when a minister spent the night in the Surrency home. While he was talking to one of the older Surrency boys, their conversation was interrupted by a thudding sound from the roof. One of the boys rushed outside and was shocked to find hot bricks falling from the sky. At the same time, the boys' married sister Clem was waiting for their father to arrive at the train station, when she beheld a bright light coming down the tracks. She knew it was not a train because there was no noise. It seemed as if the light were heading straight for her. Finally Clem could stand it no more. She ran back home as fast as she could. When she opened the front door, several hot bricks fell behind her onto the porch. Meanwhile, inside the house, the minister threw a stick into the fireplace, only to have it fly right back at him. China figurines were thrown to the floor and broken. Then the windows refused to stay closed and the door was flung open. Disembodied voices were heard as well.

Over the next few weeks, the entity inside the Surrency House continued to torment the family by playing with food and hiding articles of clothing. To the family's dismay, news of their nocturnal disturbances spread throughout the town and beyond. Some thirty thousand visitors traveled to Surrency in hopes of seeing the ghost. In 1875, A. P. Surrency decided to set the record straight by writing a letter to the *Savannah Morning News,* describing the paranormal disturbances in his home. Overwhelmed by the publicity and the manifestations, the Surrency family eventually moved away. The ghostly activity stopped altogether fifty years later when the Surrency House burned to the ground.

The Ritz Theater

The Ritz Theater is the twentieth-century incarnation of the Grand Opera House, which was built in Brunswick in 1898. Retail stores and the general offices of the Brunswick and Birmingham Railroad were also housed in the building. In the 1920s, the three-story Victorian building that was built for the legitimate stage became a vaudeville theater. In the 1930s, the Grand Opera House was converted into a movie theater under a new name, the Ritz Theater. The old theater also underwent a facelift, the brickwork on the first story being covered with carrara glass to lend it an Art Deco look. In the 1960s, the two upper stories were used as apartments. The Ritz closed its doors in 1976, but it received a new lease on life after the city of Brunswick purchased it in 1980. It was completed modernized, with the exception of the elaborate Ritz sign. The Ritz has been managed by the Golden Isles Arts and Humanities Association since 1989. Plans are now under way to transform the second and third floors into artists' studios. Some residents of Brunswick maintain that the Ritz is home not only to the arts, but to ghosts as well.

Most of the ghostly manifestations in the Ritz Theater take the form of sound. The spectral noises seem to come mainly from the side of the auditorium where the stairs lead toward the apartments on the second floor. In *Ghosts of the Georgia Coast*, Joan Stevens, executive director of the Golden Isles Arts and Humanities Association in Brunswick, recounted several of her unusual experiences in the Ritz Theater to Don Farrant. Joan said that in the fall of 1998, a technician told her that he never stayed very late in the theater, because he heard banging on the walls and footsteps headed toward the stage. A few weeks later, Joan got a taste of the fear the technician had felt when she was looking for something in one of the storage rooms on the second floor and felt the presence of someone else in the room. She was not really scared until she heard the footsteps of someone walking away from her in high heels.

Joan had a much more personal encounter with the apparition a few weeks later while shutting down the theater for the night. She was walking across the stage to turn off the lights, when she detected movement in the curtains. Then she saw a careworn woman in a plain dress walking in her direction. The woman reached out and touched Joan's face. Joan was more overcome with sadness than fear because of the tragic look on the woman's face, so she said, "I'm sorry." The woman walked off the stage and vanished. A few days later, an elderly woman and her friend visited the Ritz. The elderly woman told Joan that her middle-aged daughter Kate had committed suicide in one of the apartments. Joan suspects that the player in the tragic scene she witnessed on the stage will probably come back for a return engagement sometime in the future.

The Jacksonborough Curse

Sylvania is now the seat of Screven County, but this was not always so. Jacksonborough became the original county seat in 1797 when Solomon Gross and his wife, Mary, donated fifty acres of land on Beaver Creek to the commissioners of Screven. Unknown to the city fathers, however, Jacksonborough would be gone within fifty years. The beginning of the end for Jacksonborough came in 1820, when an itinerant Methodist preacher named Lorenzo Dow rode into town. The preacher, who called himself "Crazy Dow," was a strange-looking figure with long hair and a humpback. But he was also a powerful preacher who had earned a reputation as one of the leading evangelists. He was also known to incur the wrath of crowds who took issue with his antislavery stance and the fire-and-brimstone content of his sermons.

At the time when Dow arrived at the county seat, Jacksonborough was a rough place, where drunkenness and overall rowdiness were commonplace. George White's *Statistics of Georgia* reports that after the drunken brawls had subsided, children walking along the street often picked up eyeballs, which they placed in tea saucers. Records also show that there were no organized churches in Jacksonborough when Lorenzo Dow passed through, just "whiskey stores." On this fateful day in 1820, Lorenzo rode through town, yelling, "Repent, brethren, repent!" from his saddle. Offended by Dow's implication that the citizens of Jacksonborough needed redemption, they pelted him with tomatoes and rotten eggs. Undaunted, Dow climbed down from his horse, grabbed an iron tool, and broke open a barrel of whiskey. He probably would have been killed if a fellow Methodist and Mason named Seaborn Goodall had not hustled the preacher out of the mob to safety.

Goodall took Dow to his house on the edge of town to spend the night. Early the next morning, Dow thanked Goodall for his hospitality and started to ride back into town. He had not ridden very far before a gang of drunken ruffians blocked his way. Once again, Dow was pelted with tomatoes and rotten eggs. The mob then forced Dow to ride to the footbridge at Beaver Creek that led out of town. After shaking the dust off his feet, as Jesus Christ had instructed his disciples to do when they met opposition, Dow raised his hands to heaven and asked God to bring down the curse of

Sodom and Gomorrah upon the entire town of Jacksonborough, with the exception of the house owned by his newfound friend Seaborn Goodall.

In less than thirty years, Jacksonborough was nothing but a memory, having been destroyed by mysterious fires that gutted the stores and houses and gusts of wind that blew off the roofs. Flash floods rose up from the usually quiet creek that flowed outside of town, making the houses uninhabitable. In 1847, Sylvania became the new seat of Screven County, as well as the only town in Georgia that owes its founding to a curse.

The Dell-Goodall House, built in 1815, still stands, the only building in Jacksonborough to survive a visit from General William T. Sherman, the passing of almost two centuries, and the curse of Lorenzo Dow.

The River Monster of Darien

Stories of strange creatures living in and around the Altamaha River have circulated near Darien for centuries. One of these monsters is the Wampus Cat, a large feline said to prey on small mammals. The best known of these mythical animals is a giant water monster. First sighted by the Tama Indians, the monster was also seen by early settlers floating down the river in rafts and boats, who said it looked like a large snake that hissed when confronted by human beings. Encounters with the snakelike creature in the Altamaha River continued throughout most of the twentieth century.

A number of the 350 alleged sightings of the beast have appeared in local newspapers over the years. Several of these stories were reported in the March 15, 1998, edition of the *Augusta Chronicle*. As a rule, the creature has been seen in the deeper parts of the river between Eason's Bluff in Appling County and coastal McIntosh County near Darien. In the 1920s, a work crew of several loggers saw a "snake monster" while floating logs down the river near Doctortown. In 1935, three men hunting near Carter's Bite saw a "big snake" undulating across the river. During the summer of 1959, another sighting took place near Glennville in Tattnall County. Two officials from Reidsville State Prison were driving across a bridge when they saw what appeared at first to be a large alligator. On closer inspection, though, the animal seemed to be some sort of very large snake, possibly thirty feet or more in length. The men watched the creature for several seconds before it submerged. One Sunday afternoon in the early 1970s, a retired farmer named Benny Coursey and a friend were fishing from a boat in the river, when a "snake thing" raised its head out of the water and swam straight for their boat. Just before striking the craft, the creature rose up about twenty yards on the other side of the fishermen and plunged into the river.

A number of more recent sightings were reported in the *Darien News*. A story appeared in the February 3, 1983, issue about a strange sighting by a car salesman named Tim Sanders. While crossing the Champney River Bridge, he saw what seemed to be porpoises cavorting near the riverbank about a hundred yards away to the east. His curiosity aroused, Sanders decided to park his car and watch the playful mammals. After a minute or so, he realized that he was really watching a single reptile about twenty to twenty-five feet long. Its body crested the water with six to seven feet between humps. The creature's torso was about as thick as the girth of a man. The head seemed to have a snout. The thing swam across the river for a while, and then disappeared into a cove.

The January 14, 1993, issue told of a similar creature witnessed by Scotty Rogers. While crossing the Champney River Bridge, he saw what looked like a tractor-trailer inner tube standing on end. At least thirty feet of it came out of the water. Rogers said that one part of the monster's body appeared to be as big as a car. He regretted that he was the only one on the bridge at the time.

Another sighting occurred near the same bridge a few months later, however. Two fishermen were in a boat tied to an old power pole next to the bridge when they saw a snakelike creature swimming toward them. The men held their breath as the undulating creature swam right next to their boat, then crawled up the riverbank and slithered into the brush. This story is more difficult to dismiss than the others that have been told about the river monster because one of the fishermen was a minister.

President Jimmy Carter's UFO

A number of UFO sightings have been reported from Georgia over the years.

In 1947, three disk-shaped objects were photographed flying over Atlanta. In June 1978, a ten-year-old boy was walking with his mother to his uncle's house in Cartersville when they saw a huge, circular object hovering soundlessly in the evening sky. On March 23, 2002, a woman was driving home from Florida on I-75 with a friend. At 4 P.M., they were near Albany when they saw a bright, rainbow-colored light in the sky near the sun. They pulled off the highway and watched the strange object for ten minutes. Then the UFO emitted a bright flash that momentarily blinded the two women. When they regained their vision, they noticed that there were now three objects in the sky, flying above a squadron of planes. Soon all three objects vanished. Despite accounts such as these, Georgia did not become known as a UFO state until Jimmy Carter saw one.

On January 12, 1971, Jimmy Carter arrived at the Lions Club in Leary for a meeting. He arrived early and was standing on the landing with ten other people when he caught sight of something strange—a green and red orb shining in the sky. In an interview with the *Atlanta Constitution,* Carter said that it "seemed to move towards us from a distance, stop, move partially away, then depart. Bluish at first, then reddish—not luminous—not solid." He guessed that the UFO was between three hundred and a thousand yards away. Carter and the others stared in wonder at the unearthly object for ten whole minutes until it finally zipped away. Realizing that he had participated in an extraterrestrial event, Carter recorded his impressions on tape. "It was the damndest thing I've ever seen," he said. "It changed colors and was about the size of the moon. . . . One thing's for sure, I'll never make fun of people who say they've seen unidentified objects in the sky."

Hogzilla

In the twenty-first century, some of the most enduring legends are generated not by word of mouth, but on the Internet. A case in point is the story of Hogzilla, which first appeared on the Internet in July 2004. A hunting guide named Chris Griffin claimed to have killed a monstrous feral hog in June 2004 at the River Oak Plantation. Ken Holyoak, owner of the fifteen-hundred-acre fish and hunting preserve, said, "We killed it because we didn't want to take a chance of him getting away. Somebody else would have shot it." Holyoak said that the twelve-foot-long animal weighed a thousand pounds on his farm scales. He measured the length of the hog's tusks at nine inches. Because the meat of feral hogs is inedible and the cost of mounting the animal was prohibitive, Griffin and Ken Holyoak dug a trench and buried the beast with a backhoe. Afterward, Griffin did not even have the head of the hog to display, because it would have been too large to mount on a wall, so he began showing around a picture of himself standing in the hole next to the pig, which was suspended from the backhoe by straps tied to its hind legs. Griffin, who is six feet tall, appears to be dwarfed by the massive hog.

Before long, newspapers worldwide carried stories of the beast now known as Hogzilla. Six months later, a team of scientists from the National Geographic Channel traveled to the little Georgia town of Alapaha to conduct their own investigation. With Chris Griffin's assistance, the team located the pit where Hogzilla had been buried and exhumed the animal. They dug up a hog that measured about seven and a half feet long and weighed around eight hundred pounds. Using DNA analysis, the scientists determined that it was a hybrid of wild boar and domestic Hampshire pig.

National Geographic's disappointing findings dampened the spirits of the residents of Alapaha, but not enough to keep them from staging a Hogzilla Festival in November 2004. The celebration featured a greased-pig chase, a hog-calling contest, a parade featuring children in pink pig outfits, a Hogzilla princess, and a float carrying a Hogzilla replica. One could say that Alapaha has gone "hog wild" over Hogzilla.

Bibliography

Books

Albu, Susan H., and Elizabeth Arndt. *Here's Savannah: A Journey through Historic Savannah and Environs.* Savannah: Atlanta Printing Company, 1994.

Behrend, Jackie. *Ghosts of America's East Coast.* Birmingham, AL: Crane Hill Publishers, 2001.

Brown, Alan. *Ghost Hunters of the South.* Jackson: University Press of Mississippi, 2006.

———. *Haunted Places in the American South.* Jackson: University Press of Mississippi, 2002.

———. *Stories from the Haunted South.* Jackson: University Press of Mississippi, 2004.

Camp, Brice. *Civil War Ghosts: They Are Among Us.* Fort Wayne, IN: Sweetwater Press, 2006.

Caskey, James. *Haunted Savannah: The Official Guidebook to Savannah Haunted History Tour.* Savannah: Bonaventure Books, 2005.

Cobb, Al. *Savannah's Ghosts.* Savannah: Whitaker Street Books, 2001.

Coleman, Christopher K. *Ghosts and Haunts of the Civil War.* Nashville: Rutledge Hill Press, 1999.

DeBolt, Margaret Wayt. *Savannah Spectres and Other Strange Tales.* Virginia Beach, VA: Donning Company, 1984.

Duffey, Barbara. *Angels and Apparitions: True Ghost Stories from the South.* Eatonton, GA: Elysian Publishing Company, 1996.

———. *Banshees, Bugles and Belles: True Ghost Stories of Georgia.* Berryville, GA: Rockbridge Publishing Company, 1995.

Farrant, Don. *Ghosts of the Georgia Coast.* Sarasota, FL: Pineapple Press, 2002.

Floyd, E. Randall. *In the Realm of Ghosts and Hauntings: 40 Supernatural Occurrences from around the World.* New York: Barnes and Noble, 2002.

Guiley, Rosemary Ellen. *The Encyclopedia of Ghosts and Spirits.* New York: Facts on File, 2000.

Hauck, Dennis William. *Haunted Places: The National Directory.* New York: Penguin, 1996.

Joiner, Sean. *Haunted Augusta and Local Legends.* Florida: Lumina Press, 2002.

Bibliography

Kermeen, Frances. *Ghostly Encounters: True Stories of America's Haunted Inns and Hotels.* New York: Warner Books, 2002.

Kotarski, Georgiana C. *Ghosts of the Southern Tennessee Valley.* Winston-Salem, NC: John F. Blair, 2006.

Mead, Robin. *Haunted Hotels.* Nashville: Rutledge Hill Press, 1995.

Miles, Jim. *Weird Georgia.* New York: Sterling Publishing Co., 2006.

Montell, William Lynnwood. *Ghosts along the Cumberland: Deathlore from the Kentucky Foothills.* Knoxville: University of Tennessee Press, 1975.

Rhyne, Nancy. *Coastal Ghosts.* Orangeburg, SC: Sandlapper Publishing Co., 1985.

Roberts, Nancy. *Georgia Ghosts.* Winston-Salem, NC: John F. Blair, 1997.

Roth, David, ed. *Blue and Gray Magazine Guide to Haunted Places of the Civil War.* Columbus, OH: Blue and Gray Enterprises, 1996.

Rousseau, David H. *Savannah Ghosts.* Atglen, PA: Schiffer Publishing, 2006.

Taylor, Troy. *The Ghost Hunter's Guidebook.* Alton, IL: Whitechapel Press, 2001.

Turnage, Sheila. *Haunted Inns of the Southeast.* Winston-Salem, NC: John F. Blair, 2001.

Wallis, Kathleen. *Georgia Ghostly Getaways.* Crescent City, FL: Global Authors Publications, 2003.

Wangler, Chris. *Ghost Stories of Georgia: True Tales of Ghostly Hauntings.* Auburn, WA: Lone Pine Publishing International, 2006.

White, George. *Statistics of the State of Georgia, Including an Account of Its Natural, Civil, and Ecclesiastical History.* Savannah, GA: W. Thorne Williams, 1849.

Windham, Kathryn Tucker. *13 Georgia Ghosts and Jeffrey.* Tuscaloosa: University of Alabama Press, 1973.

Articles and Interviews

Bynum, Russ. "'Ghost Hunters' Tackles America's 'Most Haunted City.'" *Clarion Ledger.* 11 October 2005, D3.

Davig, Linda. Personal interview. 12 January 2005.

Lawson, Kimberly. "The Haunted Halls of ASU." *Augusta.* (October 2006): 58–63.

"Plans for Modern Telfair Building Meets with Opposition." *Rambler.* (December 1999): 8.

Swain, Bruce. "Georgia: A State of Paranormality." *Journal of American Culture* 11, no. 3 (Fall 1988). 35–38.

Online Sources

"About Us: Island History." *Jekyll Island Club Hotel.* Retrieved 18 January 2007. www.jekyllclub.com/about.asp?id = 13.

"Andersonville Civil War Prison: Historical Background." *Southeast Archaeological Center.* Retrieved 14 January 2007. ww.cr.nps.gov/seac/histback.htm.

"Andersonville, Georgia." *Big Bend Ghost Trackers.* Retrieved 20 January 2007. www.bigbendghosttrackers.homestead.com/files/anders.html.

"Another 'Bigfoot' Sighting in the Happy Valley Area." *Coweta County, Georgia 2005.* Retrieved 26 February 2007. www.bigfootencounters.com/articles/coweta_county05.htm.

"Anthony's Fine Dining, Atlanta: September 17th, 2005." *Historic Ghost Watch and Investigations.* Retrieved 2 February 2007. www.historicghost.com/AnthonysInvestigationsFirst.html.

"Atlanta, Georgia's Haunted Restaurant—The Ghost of Annie Barnett." *Alanjlevine.com.* Retrieved 2 February 2007. www.alanjlevine.com/annie.html.

"Augusta Arsenal." *Sherpa Guides: The Civil War in Georgia, an Illustrated Travelers Guide.* Retrieved 3 March 2007. www.sherpaguides.com/georgia/civil_war/mid_ga_east/augusta_area.html.

"Augusta, Georgia." *Classic Encyclopedia.* Retrieved 26 January 2007. www.1911encyclopedia.org/Augusta,_Georgia.

"Augusta, Georgia." *Wikipedia.* Retrieved 25 March 2007. www.en.wikipedia.org/wiki/Augusta,_Georgia.

"Augusta GA Gertrude Herbert Institute Art Vint Postcard." *eBay.* Retrieved 23 February 2007. www.cgi.ebay.com/Augusta-GA-Gertrude-Herbert-Institute-Art-Vint-Postcard_WOQQite. . .

"Augusta State University." *New Georgia Encyclopedia.* Retrieved 8 February 2007. www.georgiaencyclopedia.org/nge/Article.jsp?id = h-1421.

"Augusta State University Features Sean Joiner." *Life's Odyssey: An Extended Wandering.* Retrieved 26 January 2007. www.sjoiner.squarespace.com/press-release/.

"Augusta State University: History." *Augusta State University.* Retrieved 31 January 2007. www.aug.edu/public_information_and_publications/history/acaddays.html.

"Augusta State University: Scrapbook." *Augusta State University.* Retrieved 8 February 2007. www.aug.edu/public_information_and_publications/history/scrapbk.html.

"A Battle on the Blue and Gray Trail." *About North Georgia.* Retrieved 11 January 2007. www.ngeorgia.com/history/chickam.html.

"Benet, Stephen Vincent, House." *National Historic Landmarks Program.* Retrieved 3 February 2007. www.tps.cr.nps.gov/nhl/detail.cfm?ResourceId = 1088&ResourceType = Building.

"A Brief Review of Georgia's Civil War History." *Sherpa Guides.* Retrieved 31 March 2007. www.sherpaguides.com/georgia/civil_war/.

"Cities and Counties." *New Georgia Encyclopedia.* Retrieved 26 January 2007. www.georgiaencyclopedia.org/nge/Article.jsp?id = h-955.

"Cogdell Light." *Astronomy Café.* Retrieved 20 January 2007. www.astronomycafe.net/weird/lights/cogdell.htm.

"Could Bigfoot Be in Coweta?" *Notes from the Field.* Retrieved 27 February 2007. www.georgiabigfoot.com//index.php?option = com_content&task = view&id = 13&Itemid = 29.

Bibliography

"Cumberland Island National Seashore." *Outdoorplaces.com.* Retrieved 22 January 2007. www.outdoorplaces.com/Destination/USNP/gacumisl/.

"Curse Blamed on Angry Preacher." *History@ugusta.* Retrieved 29 January 2007. www.chronicle.augusta.com/history/pillar.html.

"The Curse of Lorenzo Dow." *RootsWeb.* Retrieved 30 January 2007. www.archiver.rootsweb.com/th/read/GASCREVE/2006–07.

"Dahlonega, Georgia." *Wikipedia.* Retrieved 5 February 2007. www.en.wikipedia.org/wiki/Dahlonega_Georgia.

"Dahlonega Gold Museum." *About North Georgia.* Retrieved 5 February 2007. www.ngeorgia.com/parks/dahlonega.html.

"Dahlonega Gold Museum Historic Site." *Georgia State Parks and Historic Sites.* Retrieved 5 February 2007. www.gastateparks.org/info/dahlonega/.

"DeKalb Buys House in Ghostly Condition." *Ghosthounds.com.* Retrieved 3 February 2007. www.ghosthounds.com/ftopict-2386.html.

"Don't Sit in the Red Velvet Chair." *Atlanta Journal and Constitution Magazine.* Retrieved 25 January 2007. www.jacquelyncook.com/Articles.redvelvet.htm.

"Dungeness and Lifestyle of Andrew Carnegie." *Acheh Times.* Retrieved 22 January 2007. www.achehtimes.com/art-humanity/dungeness.htm.

"Dungeness Ruins." *National Park Service, U.S. Department of the Interior.* Retrieved 22 January 2007. www.nps.gov/cuis/planyourvisit/placestogo.htm.

"Ebo Landing." *Glynn County, Georgia.* Retrieved 18 January 2007. www.glynncounty.com/History_and_Lore/Ebo_Landing/.

"1848 House Sold for Private Residence." *Topix.net.* Retrieved 20 January 2007. www.topix.net/forum/city/kennesaw-ga/TGBP5GU91GFTDRPD8.

"Elkins Creek Revisited." *Notes from the Field.* Retrieved 27 February 2007. www.georgiabigfoot.com//indes.php?option = com_content&task = view&id = 28&Itemid = 29.

"Ezekiel Harris House." *INUSA Tour Guide.* Retrieved 26 January 2007. www.inusa.com/tour/ga/augusta/harris.htm.

"Ezekiel Harris House: Augusta, Georgia." *Augusta Museum of History.* Retrieved 26 January 2007. www.augustamuseum.org/eh.htm.

"Fort McAllister." *Georgia State Parks and Historic Sites.* Retrieved 7 February 2007. www.gastateparks.org/net/content/go.aspx?s = 120698.120698.1.5.

"Fort McAllister." *Our Georgia History.* Retrieved 7 February 2007. www.ourgeorgiahistory.com/wars/Civil_War/ftmcallister.html.

"Fort McAllister: The Phantom Feline of the Savannah River Defenses." *Haunted Forts.* Retrieved 7 February 2007. www.militaryghosts.com/mcallister.html.

"Fort Pulaski." *Historic Preservation Societies.* Retrieved 21 February 2007. www.cr.nps.gov/hps/abpp/battles/ga001.htm.

"Fort Pulaski National Monument." *National Park Service.* Retrieved 21 February 2007. www.tybee.com/tour/pulaski.html.

"Fort Pulaski National Monument, Georgia." *Hikercentral.com.* Retrieved 21 February 2007. www.hikercentral.com/parks/fopu/.

"Fort Pulaski National Monument: Stories." *National Park Service, U.S. Department of the Interior.* Retrieved 21 February 2007. www.nps.gov/fopu/historyculture/stories.htm.

"Georgia Bigfoot Sightings." *Spacepub.* Retrieved 26 February 2007. www.spacepub.com/users/data/bigfoot/geo/geo.htm.

"Ghost Busters Investigate the Windsor." *Big Bend Ghost Trackers.* Retrieved 16 January 2007. www.windsor-americus.com/ghost/ghost_at_the_windsor.htm.

"Ghostlights." *Obiwan's UFO-Free Paranormal Page.* Retrieved 14 January 2007. www.ghosts.org/ghostlights/ghostlights.html.

"Ghostly Footsteps in the Lighthouse." *Glynn County, Georgia.* Retrieved 18 January 2007. www.glynncounty.com/cgi-bin/oaktree.pl?dbf = data.txt&ID = 00013469.

"Ghost Hounds Dig Up Stories behind Some Local 'Hauntings.'" *Ghosthounds.* Retrieved 1 February 2007. www.ghosthounds.com/press/print/gdp10-31_files/articleE42122A93F7F46E2AEF1435. . .

"Ghost Hunt: Group Examines Possible Haunted Sites for Evidence." *Ghosthounds.* Retrieved 1 February 2007. *Online Athens.* www.ghosthounds.com/press/abh-10-31-04.htm.

"Ghost Hunter Lured by Spectral Voice." *AJC.* Retrieved 16 January 2007. www.ajc.com/news/content/metro/1005/31ghost.html (1 of 4) 11/1/2005 4:05:19PM.

"A Ghost Is Found." *Pulse.* Retrieved 1 February 2007. www.ghosthounds.com/press/print/ctp-10-26-04.htm.

"The Ghost Light Phenomenon." *Strange Encounters.* Retrieved 17 January 2007. www.strange.myeyeznet/se-features-item.php/8.

"The Ghost of Kennesaw House." *Ghosts and Spirits of Tennessee.* Retrieved 21 January 2007. www.johnnorrisbrown.com/paranormal-tn/ga/kennesaw-house.htm.

"Ghost Story." *Wirenot.* Retrieved 20 January 2007. www.wirenot.net/X/Articles/aug-dec2002/G/ghoststory.shtml.

"Ghosts in the Rylander?" *Americus Times-Recorder.* Retrieved 16 January 2007. www.americustimesrecorder.com/local/local_story_005005102.html.

"Ghosts on Speed Dial." *National Review Online.* Retrieved 1 February 2007. www.ghosthounds.com/press/print/nro-10-31-03.htm.

"Ghost Trackers to Investigate Windsor Hotel." *Americus Times-Recorder.* Retrieved 16 January 2007. www.americustimesrecorder.com/siteSearch/apstorysection/local_story_223001516.html.

"Gold Museum." *60 Miles from Atlanta . . . A Million Miles from the Hassle.* Retrieved 5 February 2007. www.dahlonega.org/index.php?option = com_content&task = view&id = 61&Itemid = 102.

"Hall County." *New Georgia Encyclopedia.* Retrieved 8 February 2007. www.georgiaencyclopedia.org/nge/Article.jsp?id = h-2343.

Bibliography

"Haunted Bonnie Castle." *Research and Investigation of the Paranormal.* Retrieved 5 February 2007. www.investigateparanormal.com/bonnie _castle.htm.

"The Haunted 1848 House." *GHHT Investigations.* Retrieved 20 January 2007. www.geocities.com/Athens/Aegean/8697/pg1848.html.

"Haunted Hotels: The Windsor Hotel." *HotelChatter.* Retrieved 16 January 2007. www.hotelchatter.com/story/2006/24/225352/400/hotels/ Haunted_hotels/The_Windsor/Hotel.

"Haunted Market Pillar." *GothicMidnight.* Retrieved 29 January 2007. www.gothicmidnight.com/pillar/.

"Haunted Places in Georgia." *Shadowlands Haunted Places Index.* Retrieved 2 January 2007. www.theshadowlands.net/places/georgia.htm.

"Haunted Places in Georgia: Young Harris College." *Unsolved Mysteries.* Retrieved 23 February 2007. www.unsolvedmysteries.com/usm424314.html.

"Haunts and Spirits." *Savannah Ghosts and Locations of Savannah Haunted Hotels.* Retrieved 23 February 2007. www.bedandbreakfastsofsavannah.com/ghost.htm.

"Hay House History." *Georgia Trust.* Retrieved 22 January 2007. www.georgiatrust.orb/historicsites/hayhousehistory.html.

"Historic Oakland Cemetery: Yesterday Serving Today and Tomorrow." *About Oakland.* Retrieved 22 February 2007. www.oaklandcemetery.com/AboutOakland.htm.

"History and Archaeology." *New Georgia Encyclopedia.* Retrieved 31 March 2007. www.georgiaencyclopedia.org/nge/Article.jsp?id = h-1019.

"History of the Moon River Brewing Building." *Moon River Brewing Company.* Retrieved 14 February 2007. www.moonriverbrewing.com/restaurant.html.

"History of Piracy." *Pirates! Fact and Legend.* Retrieved 31 March 2007. www.piratesinfo.com/detail/detail.php?article_id = 44.

"History of the Pope-Walton House." *Anthony's Fine Dining.* Retrieved 2 February 2007. www.anthonysfinedining.com/history.html.

"History of the Shrimp Factory Building." *Shrimp Factory.* Retrieved 20 February 2007. www.theshrimpfactory.com/about.

"Hotels and Inns." *Ghosttraveller: Georgia.* Retrieved 20 January 2007. www.ghosttraveller.com/georgia.htm.

"Is There Bigfoot in Georgia?" *WTVM News.* Retrieved 27 February 2007. www.freewebs.com/casr/Mis%20Documents/Is%20There% 20Bigfoot%20in%20Georgia.htm.

"Jekyll Island Club Hotel." *WorldGolf.* Retrieved 18 January 2007. www.worldgolf.com/resorts/georgia/jekyll-island-club-hotel.html.

"Jekyll Island Club Hotel Ghost Story." *AllStays Ghost Hotel Guide.* Retrieved 18 January 2007. www.allstays.com/Haunted/ga_jekyllisland_club.html.

"Johnston-Felton-Hay House." *Wikipedia.* Retrieved 22 January 2007. www.en.wikipedia.org/wiki/Johnston-Felton-Hay_House.

"Kennesaw House." *GHHT Investigations.* Retrieved 21 January 2007. www.geocities.com/Athens/Aegean/8697/pghotel.html.

"Kennesaw House." *Roadsidegeorgia.com.* Retrieved 21 January 2007. www.roadsidegeorgia.com/site/kennesawhouse.html.

"Land and Resources: St. Catherines Island." *New Georgia Encyclopedia.* Retrieved 15 January 2007. www.georgiaencyclopedia.org/nge/Article.jsp?id = h-2968.

"Local Werewolf Roams Talbot County." *Columbus Georgia Online.* Retrieved 26 February 2007. www.columbusgeorgiaonline.com/harris_county18.htm.

"Longstreet Monument Unveiled in Gainesville, Ga." *Civil War News.* Retrieved 8 February 2007. www.civilwarnews.com/archive/articles/longstreet_monument.htm.

"The Longstreet Society." *Georgia Civil War Commission: The Longstreet Society.* Retrieved 8 February 2007. www.ganet.org/civilwar/longstreet.html.

"Lorenzo Dow's Curse." *Touring the Backroads of North and South Carolina.* Retrieved 30 January 2007. www.planetanimals.com/logue/DOW.html.

"Medical College of Georgia, Augusta, GA." *Picturing Augusta: Historic Postcards from the Collection of the East Central Georgia Regional Library.* Retrieved 8 February 2007. www.dlg.galileo.usg.edu/picturingaugusta/aep006.php.

"The Medical College of Georgia Project." *African Diaspora Archaeology Network.* Retrieved 8 February 2007. www.diaspora.uiuc.edu/A-AAnewsletter/newsletter13.html.

"Memory Hill Cemetery, Milledgeville, GA." *Friends of Cemeteries.* Retrieved 25 January 2007. www.friendsofcems.org/MemoryHill/Main.asp.

"New Echota." *Wikipedia.* Retrieved 26 February 2007. www.en.wikipedia.org/wiki/New_Echota.

"New Echota State Park." *Roadsidegeorgia.com.* Retrieved 26 February 2007. www.roadsidegeorgia.com/site/new_echota.html.

"Nicholas Ware." *Wikipedia.* Retrieved 23 February 2007. www.en.wikipedia.org/wiki/Nicholas_Ware.

"North Augusta's Founder—James Urquhart Jackson." *North Augusta, South Carolina: 100 Years of Excellence.* Retrieved 22 February 2007. www.northaugusta100.com/historyfounder.htm.

"Orange Hall House Museum: History." *Orange Hall House Museum Welcome.* Retrieved 20 January 2007. www.orangehall.org/history.html.

"Orna Villa." *Psychosylum.* Retrieved 21 January 2007. www.psychosylum.net/content-70.html.

"Oxford and Emory College State Historical Marker." *Carl Vinson Institute of Government.* Retrieved 30 January 2007. www.cviog.uga.edu/Projects/gainfo/gahistmarkers/oxfordhistmarker.htm.

"Panola Hall." *Eatonton Historic Homes and Buildings.* Retrieved 22 January 2007. www2.gsu.edu/ ~ wwwelf/picpages/panola.html.

"Phantom of the Plantation?" *Henry Ghost Hunters.* Retrieved 2 February 2007. www.freewebs.com/henryghosthunters/hcghinthenews.htm.

Bibliography

"Positively Ghostly!" *Ghost Talk Ghost Walk.* Retrieved 23 February 2007.
   www.asylumeclectica.com/asylum/sightseer/us/ga/savannah/ghost.htm.
"Putting Your Ghosts to Work." *Hotel Interactive.* Retrieved 16 January 2007.
   www.hotelinteractive.com/index.asp?page_id = 5000&article_id = 6493.
"'Resurrection Man' Dug Way into History." *History@ugusta.* Retrieved
   8 February 2007. www.chronicle.augusta.com/history/grave.html.
"Riverview Hotel—St. Mary: About Us." *Riverview Hotel.* Retrieved
   18 January 2007. www.riverviewhotelstmarys.com.
"Rosemary Hall." *National Register of Historic Places.* Retrieved 22 February
   2007. www.lookawayrosemaryhalls.com/RoseMain.html.
"Samuel Worcester." *Wikipedia.* Retrieved 27 February 2007.
   www.en.wikipedia.org/wiki/Samuel_Worcester.
"Screven County." *New Georgia Encyclopedia.* Retrieved 30 January 2007.
   www.georgiaencyclopedia.orb/nge/Article.
"Screven County History and Information." *State of Georgia.* Retrieved
   30 January 2007. www.mygeorgiagenealogy.com/ga_county/scr.htm.
"Screven, Georgia." *Wikipedia.* Retrieved 28 January 2007.
   www.en.wikipedia.org/wiki/Screven,_Georgia.
"Sights and Activities." *Fodor's Online Travel Guide.* Retrieved 18 January
   2007. www.fodors.com/miniguides/mgresults.cfm?destination =
   georgia_coast@613&cu.
"Six Flags over Georgia." *Wikipedia.* Retrieved 1 February 2007.
   www.en.wikipedia.org/wiki/Six_Flags_Over_Georgia.
"Spirits of Augusta's Past Linger in Hair-Raising Tales." *AugustaChronicle.*
   Retrieved 8 February 2007.
   www.chronicle.augusta.com/stories/103102/fea_haunted.shtml.
"Springer Opera House: Our History." *Springer Opera House.* Retrieved
   15 January 2007. www.springeroperahouse.org/ourhistory.cfm.
"St. Catherine's Island." *Coastal Georgia.* Retrieved 15 January 2007.
   www.coastalgeorgia.com.
"St. Catherine's Island. *Sherpa Guides: Longstreet Highroad Guide
   to the Georgia Coast and Okefenokee.* Retrieved 15 January 2007.
   www.sherpaguides.com/georgia/coast/central_coast/st_catherines
   _island.html.
"St. Simon's Island Lighthouse." *Hodnett Cooper.* Retrieved 18 January 2007.
   www.hodnettcooper.com/lighthouse.htm.
"St. Simon's Island Lighthouse: St. Simon's Island, GA—1872."
   U.S. Lighthouses. Retrieved 18 January 2007.
   www.us-lighthouses.com/displaypage.php?LightID = 55.
"Stonehenge." *Wikipedia.* Retrieved 6 February 2007.
   www.en.wikipedia.org/wiki/Stonehenge.
"Surrency Bright Spot under Georgia's Piney Woods 4/2/05."
   Unexplainable. Retrieved 17 January 2007.
   unexplainable.net/artman/publish/article_1834.shtml.
"Surrency Spook Light." *Obiwan's UFO-Free Paranormal Page.* Retrieved
   17 January 2007. www.ghosts.org/ghostlights/surrency.html.

"The Surrency Spook Light." *Rowlett Report.* Retrieved 14 January 2007.
www.strangemag.com/surrencyspooklight.html.
"Tales of Bigfoot Legend Include Sightings in Georgia—Even Clarke County."
Retrieved 27 February 2007. www.georgiabigfoot.com//index.php
?option = com_content&task = view&id = 14&Itemid = 29.
"There Once Was an Estate in Adairsville, Georgia, Which Is the Model
for the Mansion in the Novel *Saint Elmo.*" *Barnsley Gardens.* Retrieved
11 January 2007. www.mirror.org/marika.oryan/Adairsville.htm.
"Turner Films the Windsor for Its Blue Ribbon Series." *The Weekly:
Your Weekly Newspaper.* Retrieved 16 January 2007.
www.theweekly.com/news/2005/August/18/Windsor_Hotel.html.
"Unsettled Spirits Rattle the Halls inside Some of America's Oldest Hotels."
Retrieved 16 January 2007.
www.hotel-online.com/News/PR2005_3rd/Sep05_HotelGhosts.html.
"Ware, Nicholas." *Infoplease.* Retrieved 23 February 2007.
www.infoplease.com/biography/us/congress/ware-nicholas.html.
"Windsor Hotel." *Big Bend Ghost Trackers.* Retrieved 16 January 2007.
www.Bigbendghosttrackers.homestead.com/files/windsor.html.
"The Windsor Hotel: Americus, Georgia." *Big Bend Ghost Trackers.*
Retrieved 16 January 2007.
www.windsor-americus.com/ghost/ghostbusters_report.htm.
"The Windsor Is a Certified Haunted Hotel." *WALB News 10.*
Retrieved 16 January 2007.
www.walb.com/Global/story.asp?S = 5449720&nav = 5kZSQ.
"The Windsor Hotel—It Deserves a Blue Ribbon." *American Roads.*
Retrieved 16 January 2007. www.americanroads.net/Windsor.htm.
"The Wren's Nest." *AOL Cityguide.* Retrieved 26 January 2007.
www.search.cityguide.aol.com/atlanta/entertainment/the-wrens-nest
/v-103595861.
"The Wren's Nest." *Wrensnestonline.com.* Retrieved 30 January 2007.
www.wrensnestonline.com/blog/ghost-hunt-2007.
"Young Harris College." *Foundation Center: Knowledge to Build On.*
Retrieved 23 February 2007.
www.foundationcenter.org/atlanta/spotlight/at_spotlight_040104.html.

Acknowledgments

I THANK PATRICK BURNS, ANDREW CALDER, AND JULIE DYE OF THE Georgia Ghost Society; Linda Davig; Kevin Fike of the Historic Ghost Watch; Gary Greene of New Echota State Park; Rick Heflin of the Georgia Haunt Hunt Team; Rena Harp of Foothills Paranormal Investigations; Amy Keller of the Burrow County Historical Society; Cinnamon Tatum of Gulf States Paranormal; and Joey Ward of West Georgia Paranormal Research.

I also acknowledge my editor, Kyle Weaver at Stackpole Books, for his sage advice and artist Heather Adel Wiggins for her wonderfully eerie illustrations.

About the Author

ALAN BROWN IS A PROFESSOR OF ENGLISH AT THE UNIVERSITY OF WEST Alabama in Livingston. Brown has written extensively about the folklore of Alabama and the rest of the South as well. His interest in southern ghost stories has led him to write *The Face in the Window and Other Alabama Ghostlore* (1996), *Shadows and Cypress* (2000), *Haunted Places in the American South* (2002), *Stories from the Haunted South* (2005), and *Ghost Hunters of the South* (2006). When he is not teaching or writing, Brown gives ghost tours of the city of Livingston and UWA's campus.